PRAISE *for* CHISELED

What does it take to become a young man of character? *Chiseled* will help you answer this question and more. It is a great resource for guys who are ready to become men of God.

BO BOSHERS
Executive Director of Student Ministries
Willow Creek Association

In a culture that has lost the ability to initiate young men into manhood, *Chiseled* is a call to true masculinity. Young men need to be challenged to develop the grit that sees a world desperately in need of strong, fearless men who stand up and make a difference.

TOM DAVIS
President, Children's HopeChest
Author, *Confessions of a Good Christian Guy, Red Letters: Living a Faith that Bleeds* and *Fields of the Fatherless*

Thanks to Shaun Blakeney and Marcus Brotherton for taking on a project like *Chiseled*. The book title describes my journey with God over the years, and it's the very process that I pray will continue to happen in my sons' lives.

RANDY HALL
President, Student Life (www.studentlife.net)

Young men today are constantly being told that the path to manhood depends on the kind of car they drive, how much money they make, or what kind of new gadgets they own. *Chiseled* replaces lies with truth and shows young men how to refocus on what truly matters: wisdom, character, courage and compassion—the codes of real maturity.

JEFF LEELAND
Executive Director, Sparrow Clubs USA

Fun read. Deadly serious stuff.

DAVID MURROW
Author, *Why Men Hate Going to Church*

At its core, *Chiseled* challenges guys to integrate the components of what it means to become a real man into their lives. This book provides durable truths that will impact young men for a lifetime.

MICHAEL ROSS
Editor, *Breakaway* magazine

Chiseled calls young men to real manliness and toughness—falling face-down before Jesus, surrendering fully to Him, and allowing the Holy Spirit to change them from the inside out. This book will make a difference in any young man daring to mature in Christ.

DR. BARRY ST. CLAIR
Founder and President, Reach Out Youth Solutions

The brilliance of *Chiseled* is that it points young men to character instead of empty ambition; to purpose, instead of apathy; to wisdom, instead of haphazard living. It is a call to a generation in great need of clear-headed, inspiring guidance and direction.

GARY THOMAS
Author, *Sacred Marriage, The Beautiful Fight*

Shaun Blakeney was the driving force behind our high school students' new ministry to people with HIV and AIDS. He constantly pushed the students to see the world through God's eyes of compassion. His heart is tender towards vulnerable children and orphans and easily tears up as he feels their pain. He walks the walk as well as talks the talk, leading with his own life of surrender to God.

KAY WARREN
Executive Director, HIV/AIDS Initiative, Saddleback Church

I loved this book and have encouraged my leaders—male and female—to read it. Blakeney and Brotherton hit on nerves that need to be hit within the Church. If we are serious about expanding God's kingdom, we need to see young men released into action and empowered to be all that God created them to be.

DARREN WHITEHEAD
Pastor of Next Gen Ministries, Willow Creek Community Church

Shaun Blakeney and Marcus Brotherton have written a timely book about how boys can become men of character who are ready to take on the punches of life. Is there any topic of more vital concern in America today? Please read *Chiseled* and spread the word.

PAT WILLIAMS
Senior Vice President, Orlando Magic
Author, *The Pursuit* and *The Warrior Within*

CHISELED

CHISELED

A YOUNG MAN'S GUIDE *to* SHAPING CHARACTER,
TRUE TOUGHNESS, AND A LIFE THAT MATTERS

SHAUN BLAKENEY *and* MARCUS BROTHERTON

Regal

From Gospel Light
Ventura, California, U.S.A.

Published by Regal
From Gospel Light
Ventura, California, U.S.A.
www.regalbooks.com
Printed in the U.S.A.

Library of Congress Cataloging-in-Publication Data
Blakeney, Shaun, 1973-
Chiseled : a young man's guide to shaping character, true toughness,
and a life that matters / Shaun Blakeney, Marcus Brotherton.
p. cm.
ISBN 978-0-8307-4668-2 (trade paper)
1. Teenage boys—Conduct of life. 2. Teenage boys—Religious life. I. Brotherton,
Marcus. II. Title.
BJ1671.B725 2008
248.8'32—dc22

2008012569

1 2 3 4 5 6 7 8 9 10 / 15 14 13 12 11 10 09 08

Rights for publishing this book outside the U.S.A. or in non-English languages are
administered by Gospel Light Worldwide, an international not-for-profit ministry.
For additional information, please visit www.glww.org, email info@glww.org, or write
to Gospel Light Worldwide, 1957 Eastman Avenue, Ventura, CA 93003, U.S.A.

To our families:

**TERESA, AUSTIN AND
ALYSSA BLAKENEY**

and

**MARY MARGARET AND
ADDY BROTHERTON**

CONTENTS

Do you want to be an adult?

I'm not talking about the type of sweater-wearing man who sits at home Friday nights playing backgammon and drinking decaf coffee. I'm talking about the truly mature man who tries to follow Jesus Christ, a man who lives an adventure full of challenges, surprises, honor and reward.

That's what is needed today—mature men. Men who are different. Men of faith. And gaining a vision for becoming this type of man is important when you are young. Over the years, I've seen so many guys who are disinterested in their future and development as a man; and instead of growing up, they just grow older. All of a sudden they wake up at 35 years old and say, "I've been living aimlessly. I've basically been a knucklehead my whole life." Don't allow this to happen to you. Being a mature man means you see the value in leading a life worth living.

That life can begin now. There's a verse in Hebrews that is the blueprint for maturity. It describes God's Word as "full of living power, sharper than the sharpest knife" (Heb. 4:12, *NLT*). Sharp knives cut away things that don't belong. That's the pathway to becoming mature: being chiseled, letting God's Word and His Spirit shape you into who you need to be.

That's what this book is all about.

I think you'll like this book a lot. Here's why: It used to be that books for guys took two general approaches. With one, we were challenged to take the high, hard road. Guys were told to shape up, buckle down and figure out how to look good on the outside; you know: *Change your behavior*. You turned the last page and doubted you could ever pull it off or measure up. You might have been left with a sense of calling, but most times, you finished those books and felt like a klutz.

With the other approach, guys were encouraged to follow the untamed road. We were told to break free, rip off our shirts and beat our chests. That theme might have bred flexibility and freedom, but it also bred a Spring Break kind of hedonism, even from a spiritual perspective. You read those books and needed to come up for air at the end. It felt like maturity was all about living life at full throttle—and that was just a little too much. Motivating, yes. Maintainable, no.

Chiseled seeks to find the balance between liberty and responsibility.

This is not a Band-Aid book. It's not about quick fixes or stupid solutions that don't lead anywhere. This book is about real maturity; it's about building into yourself the kind of durable truths that shape you for a lifetime, not a year or two until you're out on your own for good. You will read this book and come away with an inner squaring of thought, heart and behavior. You'll turn the last page and say to yourself, "Yeah, I could be like that—and I *want* to be like that."

Shaun Blakeney and Marcus Brotherton were the right guys to write this book. I know them both and they're good men with good hearts. They don't claim to have all the answers, but they invite us along on their journeys toward maturity. I like that the maturity that they describe is a process. Maturity doesn't happen overnight; it's a progression that happens bit by bit, decision by decision, choice by choice, day by day.

Chiseled will give you the tools to build a life worth living.

Doug Fields
Author, Pastor and Youth Ministry Veteran

SOME THOUGHTS TO START WITH ON BECOMING <u>CHISELED</u>

This book is called *Chiseled*. What does that mean? Chiseled is a process as much as a result. God chisels a person—He shapes and molds that person—to maturity. When you're chiseled, the things that are flabby or immature or unneeded in your life are chipped away, and what is left is honed until you're the man God made you to be.

The chiseling process is ultimately God's responsibility. But it's something you have a hand in as well. No one will force you to become mature. It's something only you can decide that you want.

Deciding to become mature is in your best interest. When you're mature, you can handle whatever life throws at you. You've got the inside knowledge and resolve to know how to really live. When the punches of life come your way, you won't break, crumble or shake apart. There's a great verse that puts maturity into perspective:

> When I was a child, I talked like a child, I thought like a child, I reasoned like a child. *When I became a man, I put childish ways behind me* (1 Cor. 13:11, emphasis added).

Putting immature ways behind you is what this book is all about. The older you get, the more you don't want to be naïve or goofy—someone who's gullible, foolish or easily influenced. You want to develop a wise, skillful approach to living. That's true toughness; that's what it means to be mature.

To be clear, this book is not a call to act older than you are right now. If you're 18, be 18. If you're 25, be 25. There are things you can do at 18 or 25 that you can never do the rest of your life.

When I (Shaun) took my first youth pastorate at age 24, I fell into the trap of thinking that age and maturity were the same thing. I thought I had to be mature all the time—and in my mind, that meant looking the part. So I tossed aside my jeans and T-shirts and wore Dockers pants, penny loafers and a polo shirt, and I parted my hair to the side—it looked like I had just walked off the PGA tour. One day, I went to one of the local high schools for lunch. The kids wondered who this nerd was who had wandered on campus to sell them insurance. When I came home, I told my wife that I'd never do that again. I'd never be what I wasn't—mistakenly thinking that it was the mature thing to do. Over the years, I've learned to dress appropriately for whatever context I'm in. Maturity is most strongly shown when you're true to who you are yet you still know your surroundings. Today, as a pastor to students, I still wear my T-shirts and jeans when I hang out at high schools, but I save my Dockers and polo shirts for business meetings. So being chiseled is not about being older than you are now. Rather, being chiseled means that you step forward in maturity.

In this book, we're going to talk a lot about the "codes" of maturity. Why codes? Think of a code as a system to live by, a series of decisions you make that allows your freedom. Maturity is something you *develop*. It's not automatically handed to you once you reach a certain age. That's why it's important to develop your codes.

Sometimes when people hear the word "code," they think it means a rule. Like, when you become mature you have to buckle down and not have fun anymore and walk around with a consti-pated expression on your face. But God is not a white-bearded Gandalf who busts your shaft and creates indiscriminate rules to make you miserable. He sets guidelines for your life that ac-tually help you live in freedom.

It's sort of like this: A while back, I (Shaun) wanted to learn how to barefoot water-ski. So both my wife and I took lessons. A friend of ours, who's the veritable Tiger Woods of barefoot waterskiing, agreed to show us how. The thing with barefoot ski-ing is that the boat hurtles along at a ridiculous rate of speed. If you just get up there without knowing what you're doing and you fall, you'll really tank. So our friend gave us one caveat: We had to train first. Before he took us out on the lake, he showed us the ropes: We had to learn how to fall correctly, how to sit in the water with our knees in the air and lean back and put our foot on the rope correctly—so many things. It took several week-ends of training on land, then several more of working with a barefoot boom. Training stretched to nearly two months. I kept thinking, *Dude, when are we going to get behind the boat?!*

Finally the day came when my friend said that we were ready. We put on our wetsuits and got behind the boat. All that training paid off. We found that we could zip out of the water without the boom and spin around in our wetsuits and cross the wake, and everything.

That's developing a code. When you know the guidelines of how something works, and then apply those guidelines to your life, you're really free.

Think of it this way: Only when you know the code for barefoot skiing can you stay on top of the water and not bust your head wide open.

Only when you know the code for football—when you learn how to throw a spiral and correctly block, tackle and punt—can you survive and truly play the game.

Only when you know the code for learning how to drive—when you stay on one side of the road, stop at red lights and start when a light is green—can you get where you need to go.

When you know and respect the codes for being a man, you have the principles that guide you into the life you were meant to lead. You can take all the punches that life throws at you.

That's maturity.

In the pages to come, we want to examine what it means to develop the codes for true male toughness, both conceptually and practically. By "develop," we mean that we first need to know what the truths of timeless instruction say; then we need to apply those truths to our lives. What's important is how we shape our lives based on what we know.

With this in mind, each chapter is broken into the following sections:

- **Chiseled Training:** This is where we examine the truths of timeless instruction as found in the Bible. It's like we're still on the beach, and Tiger Woods is still showing us the barefoot boom.

- **Getting Punched:** This is where we look at values, beliefs, behaviors and attitudes that can harm us. This is where Tiger points out that if we're behind a boat at 55 MPH, and we wipe out, it's really going to hurt.

- **True Toughness:** This is where we see what it means to develop a wise, skillful approach to living. Tiger shows us how to point our feet correctly, how to hang on to the rope and how to eye the wake as it races toward us.

- **Developing Your Code:** This is where we put it all together—or actually, where you put it together for yourself. Nobody forces anything down your throat. It's up to you to take what you know and apply it to your life. Sometimes this reflection stage can be done alone. Sometimes it can be done in community with others. This is where Tiger hands you the rope and you decide whether or not you want to start skiing. It's up to you.

A couple of other comments about this book: First, this is not meant to be a comprehensive treatment of each subject we talk about. We're not going to tell you everything (we couldn't, even if we wanted to). Instead, we want to get you thinking and talking, hopefully with a group of trusted friends, then let you figure stuff out for yourself. We hope the material here opens up a series of good discussions in your life.

Also, some of the stories and illustrations we use are from our lives when we were in high school and college—and some are from our lives today. We've purposely included illustrations from a variety of life stages both to identify with you and to invite you into the next stage of life. Sometimes we tell stories about the stuff we've figured out. Sometimes the stories are about what went wrong.

We invite you to turn the page and begin a journey with us as we explore what it means to develop the codes for true toughness. No doubt the punches of young male adulthood are already landing fast in your life. Our hope is that we will develop chins of steel together.

Shaun Blakeney, Palm Beach Gardens, FL
Marcus Brotherton, Bellingham, WA

FACEDOWN

TRUE TOUGHNESS STARTS HERE

When I (Shaun) was a kid, I had this picture in my mind that to be a man you had to be rugged, and that meant you had to camp. Trouble was, my family never went camping. Our idea of roughing it was to check ourselves into a motel without a pool. A friend of mine had a dad who loved to camp; so one weekend, I journeyed with them into the great outdoors.

Camping was cool. You pitched your tent and split your wood and cooked over an open fire raw animals you had caught yourself. But at the end of that weekend, I was pretty much the same as I'd always been. I thought I would come back with bigger muscles, maybe even a mustache—things I was positive that all men possessed. But none of that happened. Camping didn't provide the magic ticket into maturity that I was looking for.

That's the challenge in front of us all. We know that we need to transition from *guys* into *men*, but we're not sure how. It's easy to wrongly aim for maturity by thinking that you can get there simply by going camping. Or maybe it's hunting or playing football or eating chicken wings—all of the other activities we associate with manliness.

Or maybe we define male maturity by the TV images we hold in our heads. We think that real men fight and scrap and swear, and drop funny one-liners and shoot rifles. In the end, they've gutted the villain or drilled a dodgeball at the jerk's private parts. But that's not it either.

It can be confusing, even when we hang out with older guys in a spiritual environment. Say you attend a men's function at church. You wonder if the type of behavior you see is what you want to be like when you get older. A type of forced bravado can sometimes surface—a shallow enthusiasm for how the group thinks real men are supposed to act. Conversations fall into flannel-shirted vernacular. You've got to know something about *pistons, rainbow trout* and *tee times* to fit in. You wonder why the barbecue receives the amount of reverence it does. As one younger guy at church recently asked me (Shaun), "I want to become a man, but I don't like fishing—what am I supposed to do?"

There's nothing wrong with fishing. The point is that older guys sometimes don't have it figured out either. The transition from *guy* to *man* can often be muddied. And becoming a man has little to do with the age you've reached. Even if you're 25 or 45 or 65, you can still have questions about what it means to become mature. Some guys never figure it out, no matter how old they get. They go through their entire lives acting immature. Becoming a man is not guaranteed—it's possible to be immature your whole life. Now that's a scary thought.

So why is the path to maturity so muddied?

Part of it is this: Sorry to say, but there's no magic line in the sand that signifies when you officially become a man. In Jewish culture they hold a ceremony called a Bar Mitzvah shortly after a guy turns 13. On this date, a guy is said to become responsible for his actions—socially, spiritually and legally. In other words, he's declared a *man.* (Even then there's a good chance that he's got quite a way to go.)

In Western culture, there is no one moment that signifies when you've become a man. All you have are points of reference along the way. For instance, you might get your driver's license at 16; you vote at 18; you can buy booze at 21; you rent a car at 25. In pop culture it's the joke that you become a man when you lose your virginity. But none of these "milestones" sets the deciding stamp on real male maturity.

So how do you begin on the track to maturity? How do you put immature ways behind you and develop a wise and skillful approach to living?

Strangely enough, there's one place we all need to start. That place is facedown.

CHISELED TRAINING
The Wisest Man in the World

Facedown means that you bow your heart to God and let Him work in your life. All maturity begins here.

To be clear, the goal in becoming mature is not that anyone would simply *act* wiser. It's *not* that you need to buckle down, shape up, shine up your life, or grit your teeth and try harder. Jesus scorned people who were only interested in changing behavior without changing the core of their being.

Instead, true maturity is an issue of a changed heart—of changing inner motivations, tendencies and leanings. Maturity is about becoming wiser from the inside out. And that only happens when we're facedown before God.

Think of the difference between *behavior* and *heart* like this: When you were a kid and you scrapped with your brother or a friend who came over to play, chances are your mother stopped the fight by making you apologize to each other. You didn't want to apologize, but Mom made you. Grudgingly, you both grunted out, "Sorry." Your behavior changed—you weren't whaling on each other anymore. But your hearts stayed the same—you still wanted to knock each other's heads off.

When it comes to maturity, changed behavior is not what's really important. Getting to the heart of the matter is the challenge. That's where real maturity begins. What's important is a changed heart.

A changed heart is ultimately God's business. Still, God invites us to participate in the process. God provides this crazy envelope of existence called grace. We don't do anything to get grace; it's just given to us when we ask. And God's grace is what changes us. Yet, paradoxically, God invites us along on the journey. God respects us so much that He allows us to have a hand in how we change.

Think of it this way: Developing maturity at a heart level depends on two things:

1. The power of God in our life

2. The choices we make, which demonstrate our willingness to let God's power change us

If we want to become mature, we don't just sit back and do nothing. Living by the power of God means that we ask for God's help in the process. We rely on Him to work in us—and He ultimately changes us. But we don't ignore our responsibility. We trust that He will help us live as we're meant to live. And we take steps in that direction.

It doesn't really matter what place your spiritual life is at right now. You don't have to be Joe Christian to begin the process. God welcomes anybody, whatever place he is at, to journey with Him. What's important is your willingness. You have to be willing to step further.

It is with this overarching view of grace and responsibility that a man named King Solomon set down the foundations of all that we want to talk about in this book. King Solomon was arguably the wisest man who ever lived. Every young man can develop a wise, skillful approach to living by following the instructions given in Proverbs, a book in the Bible that King Solomon wrote.

True toughness was infused in Solomon's life from the day he took the throne. When his father, King David, was just about to die, David had Solomon come to his deathbed. Propped up on pillows, the aged king breathed out his last gasps of wisdom to Solomon. "Be strong," King David said, "show yourself a man; walk in God's ways and keep his commands" (1 Kings 2:2-3).

Solomon took the charge to heart. David died soon after, and Solomon took the throne. Solomon's first tasks as king required more skill than he could ever have imagined. Adonijah, one of his evil brothers, tried to seize the kingdom from him, then tried to outsmart him by manipulating his mother, but Solomon saw through the deception and had Adonijah put to the sword. With his throne firmly established, Solomon made an alliance with Egypt, one of the most powerful countries of the day. He married the pharaoh's daughter to seal the deal, then got down to the real business of running the kingdom.

Solomon had no idea where to start. So one of his first official acts as king is recorded as worshiping God. He began his reign facedown. At a nearby worship place, Solomon offered a thousand burnt offerings as a sign of his dedication to God. God saw Solomon's willing heart, appeared to him in a dream and made a shocking statement:

"Ask for whatever you want Me to give you," God said.

Solomon must have gulped. Anything? Really? He replied with honesty: "I have no idea what I'm doing in this role. I'm only a kid and I don't know how to carry out my duties. I need wisdom."

"Good choice," God said, "and because you asked for wisdom instead of long life or wealth, I'm going to give you all that, too" (see 1 Kings 3:5-15, authors' paraphrase).

Think about that. If someone came to you and offered you anything you wanted, what would you choose? It would be easy to grab for a new SUV, a whopping house, maybe a killer job in Tahiti. But Solomon chose wisdom. Barring all else, that was the one thing he wanted most in life.

God answered Solomon's prayer for wisdom. Soon, Solomon's wisdom and understanding was described "as measureless as the sand on the seashore. Solomon's wisdom was greater than the wisdom of all the men of the East, and greater than all the wisdom of Egypt. He was wiser than any other man, including Ethan the Ezrahite—wiser than Heman, Calcol and Darda, the sons of Mahol. And his fame spread to all the surrounding nations. . . . . Men of all nations came to listen to Solomon's wisdom, sent by all the kings of the world, who had heard of his wisdom" (1 Kings 4:29-31,34). We're not sure who Ethan, Heman, Calcol and Darda were, but the implication is that they knew everything—they were the flesh-and-blood Googles of their day. Solomon's wisdom surpassed them all.

It is with this foundation of extreme wisdom that Solomon pens one of his greatest works, the book of Proverbs. He's had some life experiences by the time he writes it, for the book appears to be written to a young man, perhaps one of Solomon's own sons. In several places Solomon takes the tone of an older man instructing a younger man; for instance, "Listen, my son, to your father's instruction . . ." (Prov. 1:8) and "My son, if sinners entice you, do not give in to them" (Prov. 1:10). It's with this same attitude that we can read the book of Proverbs today.

The prologue to Proverbs (1:2-4) lays out the purpose and theme of true toughness. In the first few verses of the book, Solomon lists what the rest of the book is all about. He writes: My son, here's the unshakable toughness you want, and here's why you want it . . .

For attaining wisdom and discipline;
For understanding words of insight;
For acquiring a disciplined and prudent life, doing
what is right and just and fair;
For giving prudence to the simple, knowledge and dis-
cretion to the young—

Solomon adds that it doesn't matter if you're already wise, you can add to your wisdom (see Prov. 1:5). The book of Proverbs is for everybody, no matter what their stage of maturity.

I (Marcus) have a businessman friend, about 20 years older than I am, who takes this advice very literally. He's quite wise already, yet he continues to read through Proverbs every month—and has been doing so for years. With 31 chapters to Proverbs, he reads 1 chapter a day, year in, year out. He reads other sections of the Bible, too, but he's always in Proverbs, always adding to his wisdom.

All the stuff for developing maturity is laid out for us in Proverbs. It's there for the taking.

But the problem is that we seldom seek true toughness today. It's not in our Western culture to do so. Why?

Because wisdom just doesn't sell.

GETTING PUNCHED
The Opposite of That

Have you ever seen a commercial for wisdom?

How about an Internet site devoted to Maturity Gone Wild?

Primarily, we're taught to seek possessions and entertainment. We're a capitalist economy, and much of our life revolves around getting things, using them up, then getting more things after that.

So we're encouraged to seek cheap food when we go through the drive-thru at 1:00 A.M., and the latest greatest phones that do everything except polish the silverware. We seek testosterone-loaded trucks that take us anywhere, and teeny but powerful personal music devices, authoritative laptops and hip wrist-watches. We seek energy drinks that fling us off mountaintops, Hollywood car chases, movies about tornados that hit cities, and body wash that transports us to the red zone.

It's not that any of those things are bad. It's just that nobody markets wisdom to us. We're not used to wanting wisdom. Somehow, we have to wrap our mind around how wisdom is a good thing, then figure out what true toughness is, then learn how to develop the wise, skillful approaches to living that maturity produces. It's a greater challenge, because maturity is not automatically handed to us. That's why age is not the same thing as maturity. Plenty of guys never grow up. They have never allowed the Lord to work in their life, or taken the time or effort to figure things out. Or they've never been shown what to do by anyone older than they are. So they just keep being *kids* their whole life.

One of the greatest motivations to seek and develop true toughness is to think of what it would mean to remain unwise. Basically, you could take that same list from the prologue of the book of Proverbs and describe the opposite of gaining wisdom. It would read something like this:

My son, here's what you can expect if you never learn what it means to become mature . . .
Your life will be disorganized and undisciplined, spread out all over the place.
You won't understand anything.
You won't acquire the life you want. You'll consistently do what's wrong and unjust and biased.
People will take advantage of you.

You'll do dumb stuff all your days until you grow old and toothless. Then you'll die.

And so on.

Proverbs calls this lack of wisdom being *simpleminded*.

It's not that a simpleminded person is an imbecile. Rather, he's naïve or untaught. Picture someone whose exposure to life and wisdom has been limited. It doesn't matter if he's cool or nerdy—he could be either—but he lacks sensibility. Because of his inexperience, this person is gullible and easily influenced. He might have a certain swagger to him, but in truth, he's the type of guy a used-car salesman loves to see walking onto the car lot. He's the sucker who's born every minute. He might have friends, and even a girlfriend, but his life lacks true style. Around anybody else except other adolescents, he's socially inept. He might be the hit of the frat party, but when the chips are down, he can't be counted on. He's the guy who stays being a jackass just a little too long.

It's easy to say that this isn't you.

But simplemindedness often happens in subtle ways. We all have our guy moments. Sometimes we're just caught with our foot in our mouth, or we can't handle the pressure, or we don't know what to say or we take three steps in the wrong direction and it's hard to change course. We all need to become mature. Even *continually* become mature.

Here are some stories of guys we've worked with over the years. The names have been changed, but the stories are true. None of these guys' lives were complete messes. They all had a lot going for them. But they all experienced moments that Solomon would define as being *simpleminded*. They all went through challenging times when they needed true toughness—the wise, skillful approach to living that comes from being mature.

- The summer after Brandon graduated, he decided to go to Europe by himself to backpack around and see the sights. He had dreamed of the trip for some time. But the very day he arrived in Europe, he turned around and immediately flew home. *Too hard*, he said. He never elaborated. For some reason, Brandon couldn't handle the punches this new challenge threw at him.

- Scott headed up to Alaska one summer to work on a fishing boat. On a break, he hooked up with a girl he met one weekend. She was a lot of fun, and he said that things got "a little out of hand." But he never saw her after that weekend, so "what the heck." When Scott went back to college that fall, she tracked him down with news that she was pregnant. Now what?

- Justin repeatedly cranked up his music in his apartment. His neighbors asked him politely several times to turn things down, particularly the bass. But Justin always seemed to forget. One weekend, Justin threw a real stomper for all his friends. The music blared until 2:00 A.M. on a Sunday morning. Someone called the police. Two days later, the landlord evicted Justin.

- Gabe and Eric are high school seniors. They play video games all the time. It's not that they're bad guys; but that's all they do. ALL they do. Aside from school, sleep and the occasional tuna fish sandwich, video games are the sum total of their existence.

- Rory is 19 and has already racked up $8,500 in credit card debt. When asked what he spent the money on, he didn't know. "I guess I just eat out a lot," he said.

- Emil is 24 and has been out of college for two years. He works long hours at a brokerage firm and lives alone. He has stopped going to the college group at his church. Basically, Emil has no friends. His father never did, so why should he?

• Tyler's brother pulled a lot of strings and got him a good-paying job where he (the brother) works at a computer-chip manufacturing plant. But it meant that Tyler needed to get up at 6 A.M. every morning for the commute. Tyler worked about 10 days before he quit. He didn't have the courage to tell his boss that he was quitting. Tyler just didn't show up. His actions made it look bad for his brother. Not to mention that Tyler didn't have a job anymore, or a good reference from his employer.

These stories all point to one thing: a lack of wisdom, the type of wisdom that Solomon is talking about in Proverbs. What all these guys needed was some true toughness.

TRUE TOUGHNESS
Fear This

True toughness is not a sullen, bullying type of toughness. It's not about spitting on sidewalks or kicking people in the shins. True toughness is maturity. It's a type of true strength that helps you take the punches that life inevitably throws at you. Sometimes "punches" are the hard times that come. Sometimes punches are simply the normal ebb and flow of life. Punches are the events and activities that hit hard or that test desirable behaviors and attitudes that don't come easily. And that's most of life.

Solomon spends the 31 chapters of Proverbs talking about the ins and outs of what it means to develop true toughness.

He starts the book by bringing everything down to a bottom line. Everything he has to say hinges on one fact: "The fear of the LORD is the beginning of knowledge" (Prov. 1:7).

Fear of God is where all true toughness begins. Fear of God isn't the same as being afraid, like when you get tingles up your spine at a horror movie. Fear, in this sense, is not panic or dread. When you fear something, you typically run away from it or prepare to pound it. Fearing God is not the same thing as having a simple respect for Him, either. You can respect your colleagues or respect a nice car, but that's different than respecting a king. Fearing God means that you're in awe of Him. You recognize His power and authority. When you fear God, you sense the magnitude of who He truly is.

When you're younger, sometimes you think that it will be easier to fear God when you get older. But that's often not the case. You actually have to be more dependent on God, not less, the older you get. When you're young, you're just responsible for you. But later on, more and more people will come to depend on you. Part of our manly nature is that we don't want to let anyone down, and we don't want to show weakness. But dependence on God is one aspect of what fearing the Lord looks like.

In this season of my life, I (Shaun) have gained a new understanding of what it means to fear God. The housing market in Southern California, where my wife and I live, is just ridiculous right now. When we moved to California from Indiana, three years ago, we bought a house, which is typically a great investment. But for some reason, the market has fallen, and we find ourselves almost $100,000 in the red.

I went to our mortgage guy and asked, "What do we do?"

"Basically, you can't do anything," he said.

That's fear. When you have a huge investment like a house, there is always some risk involved. Right now, for me, that risk is big. When it comes to our house and our finances, I've got to trust God completely.

It's hard for a man to do that—to hand something completely over to God. My prayer has become, "I want to trust You fully, God, but I don't know how." The other night, I was sitting outside looking at the stars, basically just pouring my heart out to God about my housing situation. I didn't know what to do, but my eyes were on Him. That's what being facedown means. To be a true man, you trust. You say, *God, I can't do anything else but put my face to the ground and surrender to You.* That's fearing the Lord.

For me (Marcus), when I think of fearing the Lord, I remember the start of my freshman year in university. Everything seemed off-center those first few days of a new school: just a haze of maps, buildings, calendars and classrooms. I felt fear, but I felt excitement too. I could remake myself—that was one of the reasons I felt so excited. My history as an everyday high school kid was safe, and in front of me was an unsoiled slate. I could be cool this time—James Dean-cool. And who wouldn't want that? One day, soon after classes started, I saw a guy named Buck McGinness (not his real name, but close to it) in the cafeteria lunch line. Instantly, I knew that a friendship with Buck was my ticket in.

Buck wrestled in high school and looked like a rock star. He was a freshman as well, from Alaska, and knew nobody on campus either. I decided to latch on to his coolness. My plan worked. Since I had a car and Buck didn't, when he wanted to buy some shoes, we went together. Lindsie and Brandilyn (sisters of the Greek goddess Aphrodite) came with us, thanks to Buck's celebrity lure. We cruised downtown—the four of us—with me looking suave behind the wheel.

Several weeks passed. I reveled in my new status as king of the freshmen, thanks to my newfound friendship with Buck. We ate lunch at the same table, worked out at the weight room (I have no idea why I went) and went up to Vancouver, B.C., for a weekend off. On the way back, with Buck in the driver's seat of my car, I noticed flashing lights behind us. Buck got a ticket for doing 88 mph in a 55 mph zone. He mouthed off to the cop and tossed the ticket in the backseat as we drove away. He never paid the ticket either and couldn't drive in Washington State for years afterward. That was Buck. He wasn't a bad kid, just head-strong, like it's easy to be at that age. Part of me thought that getting a ticket was bold, and not paying it was the ultimate in panache. But deep down, I recognized disrespect. I didn't say anything. I didn't want Buck to think I was a geek. His pull was too powerful. He led our friendship because he was stronger; and I let him because I was using him for my identity.

About November of that year, I realized this: I genuinely liked Buck, willfulness and all. But I made a quiet turning. It was away from a friendship that pulled me down and toward who I needed to be. I needed to go my own direction, even if no one came with me. Basically, I stopped hanging around with Buck, and for the first time looked to the Lord to develop who I was to become. For me, that was the start of fearing the Lord. I made a heart-choice toward maturity. I was willing to allow the Lord to change me, even if it meant a season of solitude.

What does fearing the Lord look like in your life?

In the following chapter, we'll look at a primary building block of being facedown. This is something that nobody thinks they want, but everybody needs. Yet, when you know how much you need it, you really want it. Just before the next chapter, take some time to develop your code.

DEVELOPING YOUR CODE
Putting It All Together

When you know and respect the codes of being a man, you have the principles that guide you into the life you were meant to lead. You can take all the punches that life throws at you. That's what it means to become mature.

By "developing" a code, we mean that you first need to know what the truths of timeless instruction say, then apply those truths to your life. What's important is how you shape your life based on what you know. That's developing a code. When you know the guidelines of how something works, and then you apply them to your life, you're really free.

This is the section where you put it all together. Nobody forces anything down your throat. It's up to you to take what you know and apply it to your life. Sometimes this reflection stage can be done alone; sometimes it can be done in community with others. It's your choice.

With this in mind, take some time to think through the following questions:

1. What are some of the punches being thrown at you right now? That is, what are some of the challenges in this stage of your life that require true toughness, aka, maturity?

2. What might your life look like if you never matured? What are some of the dangers in staying where you are right now?

3. "All maturity begins facedown"—what does that mean? What might that look like in your life?

ONE THING TO THINK ABOUT:

REAL MATURITY
BEGINS FACEDOWN.

DEVELOP YOUR CODE FROM HERE.

INTERNET NANTUCKET

THE CODE OF SELF-CONTROL

The Gray Ghost is an upstart, a house shaker, a wrecker of everything tranquil; and nobody in my family knows this better than me (Shaun).

I know it at 1:07 A.M.

I know it at 3:19 A.M.

I know it at 4:42 A.M.

At least, that's what I knew last night.

Last night, like every night for the past month, the flashing red numbers on the clock by my bed drove this knowledge into me. *Flash!* I'm up again! *Flash!* I rue the day this pig in clover ever came into our life. *Flash!* I know now that getting the Gray Ghost was about the dumbest thing I've ever done.

The Gray Ghost is our new Weimaraner puppy. We're trying to potty train him right now, and with his plumbing mechanism the way it is, this means three nightly visits to the fire hydrant. If I don't get up and let him out, the smiling pooch leaves hulks and sprinkles all over the house. Three times a night! For a month! Do you know what kind of train wreck you become when you're robbed of that much sleep?!

So what in the sweet name of all that's confectionary ever possessed us to get such a beast? What was I thinking?! *Uh . . . well, a Weimaraner is a great dog, of course—it's a police breed, used for search and rescue or tracking. He's smart and loyal, and eventually he'll make a great family pet.*

Blah, blah, blah.

Why did we ever get him?

Truly, it was impulse. And the impulse was all mine.

My wife, Teresa, was the wise one in the deal; she was dead set against it from the start. Her reasoning was flawless: "We might *want* the dog," she said, "but we definitely don't *need* it—at least not right now. The family's too busy. I work. You work. The kids go to school. Who's going to take care of the Gray Ghost when we're gone all day?"

"I will," I said, nodding my head.

What an idiot I am.

Impulse prevailed, and now we're paying the price.

AS IT UNFOLDS

That's the way it is with self-control (or in this case, lack of it). If you don't have self-control, life hurts. It's as simple as that. Maybe life hurts now, or maybe life will hurt later when the results of living-by-impulse catch up with you. One way or another, it's a simple formula: No self-control equals pain.

Only with self-control can you live the life you truly want to live. Having self-control means that you focus every thought and action on your most important goals; then you slice away your lesser wants. When it comes to my new dog, my greater goal is to consistently catch enough shut-eye to be coherent the next day and be the husband, father and employee I need to be. So getting a new puppy has yanked me off this goal. My impulse has resulted in no sleep and chaotic days.

Living a life that occasionally slips out of control isn't uncommon. But there are always painful results—sometimes for you, sometimes for those you care about. When I (Marcus) was in high school, there was a plus-sized girl I hung out with once in a while. She was a pretty good friend, or had the potential to be, if only I wasn't such a jerk. One day, she wore an all-pink jogging suit to school, and in an attempt to be cool, I made some crack under my breath to another dude that the "pink elephant" had arrived.

My plus-sized friend got wind of my remark. She pulled me aside later that day. "What did you say about me? What did you say about me?!" She shook her head and repeated the same line, obviously wounded by my carelessness. I just stood there, mouth flapping, looking for all the world like the *guy* I truly was at that moment. I wanted to take back what I had said, but there was no way I could. My lack of self-control in the joking-around arena hurt this girl. There are times when saying you're sorry isn't enough. The damage had already been done to my friend no matter how I tried to remedy the situation.

Living a self-controlled life is absolutely essential to being the man you want to be. Try living a life with no self-control for a while and see how far it gets you. When you're not self-controlled, you're out of control. You're goofy, crazy, all over the place, thoughtless, insensitive, hurtful. You create chaos; you end up looking stupid; you're mocked and ridiculed; you lose the respect of yourself and others. Hey, at the very least you're up all night and blurry the next day.

In contrast, think of self-control as the vehicle for achieving your goals. Do you want to be a man who is truly a good friend to others? One vital means to get you there is the exercise of self-control. Do you want to be a man who's strong, robust, worthy of respect? Again, the means is self-control. Do you want to be a man who accomplishes extraordinary things in life? Only by developing self-control will you head up that path. Self-control brings freedom. It lets you do what you truly want to do.

Self-control can play a role in a lot of areas. It affects:

- *Your sexuality.* Most guys struggle with this. There's this fire inside of you that always smolders under the surface. Risky. Unpredictable. Dangerous. Maybe it's tough for you to walk by a magazine stand without pausing to thumb through the back row. The Internet with all its lures is always just a click away. Maybe you and your girlfriend are going too far too fast.

- *Your words—what you say (or don't say).* Maybe you blurt out words at the wrong times. Or you'll go any distance to tell the old locker room joke about the farmer from Nantucket. Or you always have strong opinions and never hesitate to voice them. Or you have a hard time telling people (or showing people) exactly what you think of them.

- *Your identity.* Maybe you can't pass up a joint at a party. Or with a certain group of friends you find that you're not quite the same kind of person as when you're not with them—these friends hold a certain sway over you. Anytime you're with them, it's trouble.

- *Your responsibility level.* Maybe anytime something goes wrong, it's always "I was having an off-day" or "That's someone else's job." You pass the buck but never own up to your own stuff.

- *Your anger.* Maybe you often express frustration by blowing up. And when you blow up, you only make things worse.

- *Your time management.* Maybe when it comes to homework or chores around the dorm, you're the guy who always finds something else to do.

• *Your style of helping people.* Sometimes relationships with needy people become a problem when you fail to set proper boundaries. You're always at the beck and call of someone. Whenever they bleed, you're always there to rescue them.

Developing self-control is at the core of the life you want to lead. It's at the core of the man you want to become. Self-control means that by the power of God, you take responsibility for your life.

It's something every guy needs.

But no one ever said that developing self-control was easy.

CHISELED TRAINING
A Long List of One Thing

The wisest man in the world, Solomon, stumbled at more than one point when it came to self-control. Thankfully, we can learn from his life.

One of Solomon's challenges was that he had limitless opportunities to give in to his impulses. He was the wealthiest, most lavish, most celebrated monarch Israel had ever known. Fame. Fortune. It was all his. He owned a swanky palace. He had a harem of a thousand babes. Everyone sought his audience. All the world's offerings were his—any time he wanted.

Not a good climate for developing self-control.

And yes, Solomon dabbled in excess. Another book that Solomon wrote, Ecclesiastes, talks about some of his life experiments. A single verse sums up how he lived for a time: "I denied myself nothing my eyes desired" (Eccles. 2:10).

Did you catch that? Solomon denied himself *nothing.* What would it mean for a guy to live this way?

For a while it might be real blast. Picture taking five of your best friends on a first-class trip anywhere you wanted, in your own private jet. Want to stop at a major league baseball game? Remember, you're denying yourself *nothing*. You could rent out the entire Safeco Stadium if you wanted, just for you and your friends. Want a few new SUVs for the ride home? Catch a limo down to the Hummer dealership and pick out seven new ones for each of you—a different color for each day of the week.

But remember, without self-control, the only voice you're heeding is the voice of desire. You're not listening to the aspirations of your greater goals. You're denying yourself *nothing*. That means you're living only on impulse. You're certainly not listening to any murmur of conscience. You're not heeding morality or justice or the call to treat people fairly or any of the freeing commands in Scripture. Psalm 119:32 reads, "I run in the path of your commands, for you have set my heart free."

So, feel like getting out a little aggression? Bust a bottle over the guy's head next to you at a party and see what happens. Feel like mouthing off to your professor? Tell him exactly what you think of him and see what kind of grade you get. Feel like testing the speedometer on your Acura? Rev up to the mutton-head next to you at a stoplight and stomp down a school zone. Feel like a down-and-dirty? Cruise around your city's red-light district for a while and see what you catch. Feel like a boost? Dissolve a little slip under your tongue for a night of up and up, and dance the night away.

What will happen?

Any time you live by impulse, there are consequences. That lifestyle was completely available to Solomon. It was a life without *any* boundaries. Solomon tried it for a while, and he knew firsthand what it meant to live a life based on excess and impulse. That's what much of the book of Ecclesiastes shows.

His conclusion?

Meaningless! Meaningless! Everything is meaningless! (Eccles. 12:8).

Probably much of Proverbs was written after Solomon lived through the experiments of Ecclesiastes. Wisdom often comes from our mistakes. In Proverbs, Solomon often writes as if he's a father talking to his son. Solomon wants young men to avoid the pain of living a life out of control.

Consider:

- A lack of self-control can cause you to lose your way, even die (see Prov. 5:22-23).

- Fools lack self-control and show their annoyance at once. Wise living means that you have the smarts to overlook insults (see Prov. 12:16).

- Self-control means watching what you say. You don't just blurt out any old thing (see Prov. 13:3).

- Conquering yourself is better than conquering a city (see Prov. 16:32).

Toward the end of Proverbs, Solomon sums up all he knows about self-control like this:

Like a city whose walls are broken down is a man who lacks self-control (Prov. 25:28).

In Solomon's day, a city's walls were its fortification—its strength, its core. A city's walls allowed the people within to hold jobs and raise families and do recreation and enjoy the lives they wanted to live.

Can you picture a city with broken-down walls? Chunks of rubble block the path, hindering everybody's daily life. Weeds grow around the ruins and look ugly, even laughable. There are no defenses or safety. Any enemy who wants to can swoop in and wreak havoc. Identity is lost. It's not a city anyone is proud of. It's just a pile of debris.

A guy without self-control is like that city. Without self-control, you're hindered. You can't live the life you truly want. You're defenseless. Anything you value can be stripped away from you and stomped on. You lose strength. You lose identity and a healthy type of pride. You lose your self-respect. You lose your freedom.

An additional picture of self-control is offered later on in Scripture. Solomon didn't write this part, but it goes hand-in-glove with what he's saying.

In the New Testament, the apostle Paul made some notes for a young preacher named Titus. Paul was training Titus how to develop a wise, skillful approach to living. Part of that training meant that Paul had left Titus alone on an island called Crete to continue the work of leading a church there.

Crete was no sheltered community. One history book describes ancient Crete as "[filled with] naturally belligerent, argumentative people; uncontrolled, resentful of authority and partial to the bottle."[1] Picture Cancun at Spring Break, or any major university's Greek Row on a Friday night. That was Crete in Titus's day.

In the opening of the letter that Paul writes to Titus, Paul tells him to teach the people he cares for how to truly live. Paul lays out a list of specific codes for each age group in the congregation to watch for and develop. For the older men, Paul lists seven areas: be worthy of respect, sound in faith . . . that type of thing. For the older women, Paul lists another four areas. Then for the younger women, Paul lists another seven.

Here's the funny thing—last on his list come the directives for the guys. And when he gets to the guys, the younger men, Paul's list is cut short to only *one* thing:

Encourage the young men to be self-controlled (Titus 2:6).

One thing: self-control.

Paul knew what it's like to be a guy.

Guys are creatures of impulse. And developing the code for self-control is the vital thing at the core of who we need to be.

So what keeps us back?

Excuses.

That and the crazy belief that self-control means you can only drive a Volvo.

GETTING PUNCHED
Whatever Kind of Car You Drive

What are the values, beliefs and behaviors that harm us when it comes to developing self-control? Two main punches come at us fast.

The first punch is the excuses we make. Anytime we don't develop self-control, we tell ourselves things like:

- Being self-controlled is no fun.
- Why try to be self-controlled? I am just going to fail anyway.
- I'll be self-controlled later, when I'm older.
- People just have to like me the way I am. I'm a goofball (or a free spirit, or cool, or a great street racer, or whatever). This is me—love me, world.
- It's too hard to change.
- I don't want to change.
- I can't change.
- No one is going to tell me what to do with my life—including me.

I (Shaun) know what it means to go through the list of excuses. In my junior year, I had some friends who were a lot of fun, but always a bit too much fun, if you know what I mean. They were the guys that everybody thought were hilarious, but they were also always in trouble. Any type of big prank or problem in school could be traced back to them.

I grew up in Merritt Island, Florida, a small NASA town about five miles from Kennedy Space Center. Everybody's dad was educated and had a good job. Most of the kids I knew had money and all the stuff they could ever want. It was not an area known for limiting excess.

One weekend, these same hilarious friends from school planned a scavenger hunt for all over the island. Everyone at school got a list and was supposed to catch a ride and speed all over the place to get the things on the list and then cross them off or accomplish some prank before a certain time limit. Things like: You had to go through the Wendy's drive-thru and ask for a fork only. Or you had to go to the Banana River and take a picture of yourself standing in the water with your shirt off. The list looked innocent enough at first.

I told my mom that I wanted to go on the hunt, but both she and my dad said no—they knew who was planning it and probably how it would turn out. I was mad. I went to my room to think things over.

I knew that going out with the hilarious guys wasn't the best thing to do. But if I went, everyone would know that I had gone with them, and it would be the cool thing back at school on Monday. So I felt divided. I could have gone. I could have sneaked out of the house. Fact is, after you reach a certain age, every decision you make is up to you, regardless of what your parents say. You always own the decision to be obedient to your conscience.

I remember sitting on my bed, the open window next to me. It wouldn't be the first time I had snuck out at night. My mind rolled around a list of excuses. I doubt if I articulated them exactly like this, but it was essentially stuff like:

- Why be self-controlled? I'm young—I'm supposed to have fun.

- None of these other guys is staying home. Why do I have to?

- What do my parents know anyway?

That type of thing.

But for that time, at least, I chose self-control. I chose to be obedient to my parents. I chose not to go.

It turned out to be the right decision. The next day, we read in the newspaper that more than $200,000 in damage was reported due to the scavenger hunt. More than thirty carloads of kids ended up participating, and things got crazy. Booze flowed. Billboards were ruined by graffiti. The microphone at Wendy's was ripped out of the ground. It was a real wild night.

What excuses do you tell yourself to keep from developing self-control?

Another punch is delivered by the notion that being self-controlled means being tied in a knot all the time. It's often what people imagine when they envision self-control, but it's the wrong picture.

True self-control is not about weighing your life down with a series of petty rules. Self-control is not about stifling yourself or being less than you are or ingesting into your gut a lengthy series of moral lectures or tying your hand to the bedpost so that you won't masturbate at night.

When you think about a man who's self-controlled, sometimes you envision someone who's restrained. He has curbed his appetites. He's nice all the time. He drives a brown four-door

Volvo and wears a button-down shirt at the beach. Somehow this man has become bloated on kindliness; his main goal is only to get along with everybody. The word "tepid" comes to mind when describing this man. Maybe even "spineless." He's controlled in the sense that he has bound up all his emotions. He's wound up tighter than a three-dollar watch.

I (Marcus) am sometimes tempted in this area. I grew up in Canada, where adults aren't known for being overly expressive. We're known as peacemakers, kind of like Switzerland. American history has wars and revolutions and blood and guts. Canadian history has polite conversations and document signings. We shout only at hockey games. The rest of the time we whisper like we're at a funeral.

When I was first married, I found out this doesn't work for very long. My sweet wife has Texas and Southern California in her roots. Her extended family hugs and shouts and argues and laughs out loud—everything Canadians don't do. So with me being so overly nice all the time, and my wife much more in touch with her true feelings, she and I found ourselves in an argument almost every week.

I take responsibility for that. I was fueled by the wrong type of self-control. I wasn't talking, or being truthful. Any new marriage has its share of adjustments, but mistakenly, I thought being self-controlled meant holding everything inside. Nobody is that nice. Including me. So I boiled over.

Over the years, I have learned to talk about adjustments when they happen so that they don't build up. If you're ticked, you've got to tell your best friend when it happens. Being self-controlled doesn't mean holding it all inside all the time.

I doubt if Jesus Christ would have driven a brown four-door. He was the epitome of self-control, yet He was far from a button-down sort of man. Jesus was dynamic, outspoken, someone who didn't mince words. He was a bold and sharp-edged leader, decisive, tough and fair. Prostitutes kissed His feet. He threw over the money changers' tables and booted them out of the Temple. Once, He walked into a dinner party and immediately began insulting His host (see Luke 11:37-53). What kind of wild self-control was that?

Here's the secret: Self-control doesn't mean being weak, mild, repressed or tied up tight.

Self-control means being strong and wise, knowing your true feelings and expressing them appropriately. Self-control means that you have a sound mind; you're not out of control. Your passions and energies aren't curbed, but they're channeled in a direction that brings the greatest possible good to yourself and others.

So how do you develop that type of true self-control—not the uptight type of self-control? We'll talk about that in the section below.

TRUE TOUGHNESS
What Mike Tyson Only Wishes

Some people think that the way you develop self-control is to always say no. No dessert. No making out with your girlfriend. No driving over the speed limit. No shouting. No smoking cigars. No beer. No carousing. No. No. No. Always no.

Other people think of self-control as always saying yes. Yes—follow your passions. Yes—make the leap. Yes—live the wild, free life. Yes—jump into the great adventure. Yes—suck out the marrow of life and drain it to the core. Yes. Yes. Yes.

Truly, self-control is more like an exchange. You give something and you get something in return. Sometimes that means saying no. Sometimes that means saying yes. You exchange your impulses for your greater goals.

The Bible presents this type of exchange as a paradox. It's something that seems contradictory but really isn't—like the world's toughest prizefighter talking like Mickey Mouse on helium; or the new Dodge Durango, which is actually a minivan in disguise, but actually sort of cool.

The Bible says that self-control originates as a fruit of the Spirit (see Gal. 5:23). So self-control comes from God, as your heart is turned toward Him.

That's the paradox: To gain control over your actions, you actually give control to God. Want to develop self-control? Pray for it, and God, as you follow Him, gives you the power to exchange your impulses for your goals.

The crazy thing about living a life that's in God's control is that God never asks you to relinquish responsibility. For instance, God may ultimately control your life, but when the alarm clock goes off in the morning, your brain still needs to tell your feet to go stand in the shower. It's God's *ultimate* control working in harmony with our *personal* control. God's in charge, yet we are always responsible for our actions.

So each morning, I (Shaun) go work out at a gym. There are always tons of ladies there dressed in the tightest, skimpiest workout clothes. Human nature says, "Look at the ladies, talk with the ladies, have long conversations with the ladies."

But self-control tells me, "Make the exchange."

I exchange my impulses for my greater goal. Self-control says to look the other way and trade the urge to gawk for the better plan of connecting with my amazing wife when I'm back home. God is in charge of my life—He gives me the power, yes, but I am also responsible for turning my head.

So, is my self-control at the gym all up to God?

Absolutely.

And is self-control at the gym still my responsibility?

Yep.

That's the paradox.

Where do you fit into all this?

Once you've developed the code for living facedown, like we talked about in the first chapter, how do you develop the code of self-control? How do you make the exchange? Let's walk through some of the pieces of this process together.

The first piece is knowing where you're out of control. Lots of people are all over the place, but it's not always easy to see that. So maybe this means that you need to ask some of your trusted friends, or a mentor, how they see your life.

Questions to ask include:

- Do you see me as an impulsive person? If so, in what areas?
- In what areas do I appear out of control?
- Do you see me creating chaos wherever I go?
- If I continue in a particular course of action, whatever it is, will I be in danger? Am I creating patterns right now that will be a problem later on?

Then, start facedown. Make prayer the first action you take. Give over to God whatever area in which you lack self-control. Wave the white flag. Follow His leadership in your life.

Your prayer can be as simple as:

> *God, I know I'm out of control in this area.*
> *I give You the ultimate control.*
> *Please help me in this area.*
> *Give me the power to exchange the harmful*
> *way for the better path.*
> *Amen.*

Another important piece is accountability. Accountability means that you don't walk the road alone; you enlist a band of brothers around you to help fight the battles. Together, you develop the system that ensures your success.

So maybe there are questions that you and your accountability partner will talk through each week to break an out-of-control pattern in your life. Or perhaps you and your accountability partner will brainstorm how to create a system of checks and balances to get your life back in control. Maybe it means saying yes to certain things. Or maybe it means saying no. You figure it out together. What exchanges do you need to make to reach your goals?

One note about accountability partners: Your best buddies are a necessary component in the accountability system. If you can't talk to your best friends, who can you talk to? But an additional component in the accountability system is being responsible to someone who's not your best friend. Why?

Just out of college, I (Marcus) was dating a girl and wanted to stay the course of purity with her. I talked with a good buddy who sort of put his arm around my shoulder and said, "Don't sweat it, man. Me and Janie weren't angels before we were married." (Again, Janie wasn't her real name, but you expect that by now in this book.)

My buddy's offhand response didn't pack the wallop I needed to hear. It didn't challenge me. It just sort of let me off the hook.

So I went to an older man in my church, one of the deacons who sat on the board of directors, and asked him to meet with me once a week and ask me any question he wanted about my dating relationship. He worked for the border patrol, was used to asking people tough questions and, honestly, the guy scared the ca-ca out of me.

Reporting to him provided the type of accountability I needed. Find someone who will tell you what you need to hear, not what you want to hear. Accountability doesn't always need to be comfortable; it needs to work.

DEVELOPING YOUR CODE
The Exchange in Action

Success in the area of self-control means developing a plan that is tailor-made to the specifics of your life. So let's get right down to business. Work through these questions by yourself or with a small group of trusted guys, or with a mentor, one on one.

1. What does it really mean for a young man to be self-controlled? What are the benefits to living a life that is self-controlled, and how might you mess things up if you're not?

2. What are the greatest areas right now in which you struggle with self-control? Can you give an example?

3. What steps do you need to take today to ensure success in this area?

Note

1. David Alexander and Pat Alexander, eds., *Eerdmans Handbook to the Bible* (Grand Rapids, MI: William B. Eerdmans Publishing Company, 1983), p. 624.

ONE THING TO THINK ABOUT:

SELF-CONTROL IS AN EXCHANGE. (YOU EXCHANGE YOUR IMPULSES FOR YOUR GREATER GOALS.)

DEVELOP YOUR CODE FROM HERE.

STEEL GIRDERS
THE CODE OF INTEGRITY

Special Agent Shaun Blakeney. It had a good ring to it, I thought. As a freshman at Florida Christian College, my career was set. After I graduated, my plan was to join the Bureau, wear a three-piece suit, carry a gun and flip open a badge as I said, "Shaun Blakeney . . . FBI."

Wait.

Either that or be a youth pastor.

When I was 19, I landed a job as a part-time youth minister at a church about three hours away from my college. The ministry was all geared around weekends. I'd hop in my Honda Civic after classes each Friday, drive to the church, lead a fun event Friday night, hang out with students all day Saturday, teach a Sunday School class Sunday morning, hold youth group Sunday night, then zip back to campus late that evening for another week of school. It was hard work, but I loved it. The students were really growing. I was learning a ton myself.

At first, things were as smooth as Marvin Gaye's music. But one day, about halfway through my first year, everything hit the fan. I was in the foyer before church, with the senior pastor, shaking hands with everybody as they filed in.

"Good morning," said the senior pastor to a woman as she entered.

"Well, it was until I saw your ugly face," she sneered. She looked as if she had just downed a bottle of vinegar. Seriously— that's what the woman said, word for word. And she wasn't smiling.

My mouth hung open. So did the senior pastor's.

What in the world was happening?

Turns out she was only the first in a small herd of sour people to file into church that morning. They were leading a charge to crucify the senior pastor, and they were out for blood. They wanted a flashier guy in the pulpit. Someone younger and with more pizzazz. They wanted my boss canned—now.

The senior pastor dug in. He told the sour folks he wasn't going anywhere. Almost overnight, the church split. All the folks who wanted a younger pastor left in a bunch for a church that had one.

A week after the exodus, the senior pastor called me into his office. The discussion was all about staff unity. "We really need to stay close through this, Shaun," he said. "You watch out for me, and I'll watch out for you." I nodded. Absolutely, I'd support my boss through this hard time.

We limped along for another three weeks. My boss called to say the church elders were holding a meeting that upcoming Friday night, and I needed to be there. I didn't usually go to elder meetings, but no problem. I would lend my support in whatever way I could.

The elder meeting was all about coins and cash. With the church now half empty, we had hit a financial snag. The treasurer addressed the senior pastor: "We're going to have to ask you to take a pay cut," the treasurer said.

The senior pastor shook his head and said, "Absolutely not." Then came the words that floored me. It was a directive—not a suggestion, a question or a request. "You don't cut my salary," said my boss. "You let Shaun go."

I was sitting right next to him. Did I catch that correctly? He just announced to the board that he was firing me. Where was all the talk about supporting each other through the hard times? His remark speared me to the wall.

"No need to release me," I said. "I quit."

And I did. I walked out of the meeting and crawled into my car. My first job in pastoral ministry was officially over. Crying, I pulled over at the nearest payphone (those were the days before cell phones) and called my dad for advice. "Shaun, people can be like that under pressure," he said. "The Lord will show you what to do."

On the long drive back to college, I started praying like never before. "God, what just happened? I've given my life to you. This was the first ministry job I've ever held—and it all blew up. Will it always be this way? Maybe I should try the FBI."

I wish I could say that I gained understanding, or even that I felt a bit better right then. But I didn't. I crawled through about eight months when I never wanted to be in youth ministry again. I was angry at the people who had destroyed the church. I was disillusioned with the senior pastor. His integrity was in question, as far as I was concerned. He had told me to watch out for him, and promised he'd watch out for me. But when the chips were down, I was out of a job.

AS IT UNFOLDS

Has someone's lack of integrity ever hurt you?

Maybe it was a betrayal. Someone insisted that he had your back. But when the pressure came, he crumbled, leaving you exposed.

Or perhaps it was a deception. Someone was adamant about a block of so-called truth. You bought into whatever he was selling. But time passed and his story turned out to be a load of cock-and-bull. You ended up holding the bag.

Perhaps the issue with integrity was your own. You knew that your heart should be heading one way, but you flirted with the other direction, a dangerous path.

When integrity doesn't exist, people get hurt.

That's why integrity is so needed.

Having integrity means living an uncompromising adherence to ethical principles. Forthrightness. Straightforwardness. It's a state of being whole or entire. It's a diamond-solid life, a life that doesn't crack under intense pressure. Integrity is soundness, an ability to deliver on promises. Think of integrity as a refusal to be false. Or a pledge to be upright. It's what you want the people around you to have. It's what you absolutely need in your own life to become the man you want to be.

A person's integrity can show up (or crack) in a lot of different ways. Consider these scenarios:

- You're up for a promotion. It means better hours and more money, but you've got to bend the truth to get the gig. Is it worth it?

- You need to make a certain grade to keep up your GPA. You haven't put in the time you should on a test. Do you write the answers on your palm? Or are you willing to get the grade you actually deserve?

- You sponsor a child through an international relief organization, which costs you $38 per month. One month you're a bit short, so you ditch the payment. You would have had enough, but there was this amazing shirt you just had to buy.

- Someone takes you out for lunch and offers to pay. Do you order what you normally would, or do you call for appetizers, the prime rib and Chocolate Thunder from Down Under for dessert? Does the knowledge of somebody's expense account make your eyes go big?

• You promised a female friend to go to a concert with her. She's nobody you'd ever date seriously, but you always have fun whenever you're together. Out of the blue, along comes a chance to go to the concert with another girl—the girl you've been pining over for months. Do you break your first commitment?

• You're getting minimum wage at a job you hate. Do you work your best or slack off?

Questions like these, and even tougher situations, continually emerge in the life of someone who wants to be a man. Do you take the honorable path? Do you stay solid? Are you unswerving in your commitment to do the principled thing? Or do you crumble? Fade away? Trade your integrity to look cool or keep a dollar in your pocket or achieve a place or position you didn't earn?

Developing integrity is not a one-time decision. It's a way of life, a series of decisions you continually make. It means constantly aligning your heart with what you know is true, noble, pure, admirable and right.

So how do you know if you have or haven't developed the code of integrity? How do you know if you're being a "guy" or a "man" in this area?

Usually, your conscience shouts at you if you haven't shown integrity. And what does it shout?

Dread.

Do you know what dread sounds like? I've been there. Just out of college, I (Marcus) dated a girl on and off for a few months. In my heart, I knew that I shouldn't be dating her. I had resolved to get serious only with someone who had the same spiritual values as me. This girl was clearly heading in a different direction.

Yet the attraction was strong. She had it all: a sense of humor, a witty brain, hair, eyes, smile—enough to keep a team of poets busy for weeks. That's the voice of temptation—do you date someone you know you shouldn't, even when everything inside you screams yes? The relationship was never going to work out long-term, and we both knew it. So what did I do?

Like an idiot, I kissed her. When the date was over that night, I took her back to her place and then went for a walk by myself. The blare of dread was so loud that I knew I had stepped over the line when it came to my integrity. The tension in my gut tied me in knots. I went back to my apartment and actually puked. So much for a fun evening.

That's how integrity works. When you're not living a life of honesty, you're a shambles inside. You might not always vomit like I did, but you can hear the dread in your soul. Dread is real. You know that you're not being true to what's right. You know that you've got to make the honorable decision, no matter what the cost. So do you do it? For me, integrity meant not dating this girl, as phenomenal as she was. It was the hard choice, the honorable choice, but I made it. It was the choice a real man would make.

Developing integrity is at the core of the life you want to lead. It's at the core of being the man you want to become. Integrity means that by the power of God, you take responsibility for your life and live by a code that doesn't waver.

It's something every guy needs—and keeps needing the older he gets.

CHISELED TRAINING
Bill Gates's Cows

In the book of Proverbs, King Solomon had a lot to say about integrity. Funny thing, because the older Solomon got, the more his integrity took a beating. Wise as Solomon was, he let his integrity crumble as the years rolled on.

Solomon's downfall was women—lots of them. He got hot and heavy with more and more wives and mistresses—all babes, undoubtedly—until there were about a thousand in his harem. Remember, he was the richest, most powerful king ever.

His relationships were mostly with women who worshiped other gods besides Jehovah. At the end of his life, the once-wisest king of Israel spent most of his remaining days prostrate in the temples of false idols, making sacrifices to statues of wood, bronze and stone. Sadly, the Bible records that as he grew older, "[Solomon] did not follow the Lord completely, as David his father had done" (1 Kings 11:6).

Years before his death, when Solomon penned much of Proverbs, it's almost like he can sense how precarious his integrity is, how easy it is to let integrity slip away. He wrote, "Let love and faithfulness never leave you; bind them around your neck, write them on the tablet of your heart" (Prov. 3:3). Those are strong words—tie integrity around you tightly, he says, before it gets away from you. Hold on to integrity for dear life.

Elsewhere in Proverbs, Solomon wrote about the necessity and the benefit of having integrity. He knows what's right; he just doesn't follow it his whole life.

"The integrity of the upright guides them, but the unfaithful are destroyed by their duplicity," he wrote in Proverbs 11:3.

"Better a poor man whose walk is blameless than a fool whose lips are perverse," Solomon wrote in Proverbs 19:1.

Solomon knew the benefits of integrity, even though he let integrity slide. A predecessor of Solomon's shows us what it means to live a life of integrity—both possessing it and keeping it when the punches of life come at you fast.

That man was Job.

Job was no ordinary guy. Think of Job as an ancient-day Bill Gates. Job was the Mr. Megabucks of the era. He had 10 children, a sure sign of a wealthy man, and he owned 7,000 sheep, 3,000 camels, 500 yoke of oxen and 500 donkeys. He had it all. The Bible says, "[Job] was the greatest man among all the people of the East" (Job 1:3).

Owning a bunch of camels and sheep might not mean anything to us today, but imagine instead that Job owned 7,000 Porsches, or 3,000 jet skis, or 500 Harleys. Job was the Jay Leno of the ancient agricultural world. Instead of collecting classic cars, he collected classic cows. The man had bucks.

Along with his vast wealth, Job had integrity. He led a straightforward life, a life without dread. He was "blameless and upright; he feared God and shunned evil" (Job 1:1). Even Satan recognized Job's integrity, as ironic as that sounds.

One day, Satan came to God and proposed a wild spiritual contest. Their conversation went something like this:

Satan: Hey God, you got anybody I can mess with?

God: Have you considered Job? He's blameless and upright. You'll never destroy him.

Satan: You're just mollycoddling Job. You've given him a sweet life. Take away all his Porsches and see if he stays true.

God: Fine. Give it your best shot, Satan. I know Job's as solid as a steel girder. He won't crack under pressure.

The contest began. In wave after wave, all that Job owned was quickly destroyed by Satan. Raiders came and stole his animals. Lightning fell from the sky and zapped his goods. The roof fell in on a house where his kids were staying.

Job was soon a wrecked man.

Yet his integrity emerged intact. Even after all the calamity, Job was able to fall to the ground in worship and declare:

The LORD gave and the LORD has taken away; may the name of the LORD be praised (Job 1:21).

That's integrity—holding fast to God and His ways, even in the midst of extreme pressure. Integrity means that even though hard things happen, you're still praising God. You're living a God-directed lifestyle every day, no matter what happens. That's exactly what Job did—he had every reason to curse God and die, but Job held his ground.

So Satan upped the stakes. He came back to God and asked Him if he could ruin Job's body. God agreed. Soon, Satan inflicted Job with painful boils all over his body. Job was in so much pain that he actually took a piece of broken pottery and scraped his skin, desperate for relief.

Everyone around him gave up. Job's integrity was tested by those he loved dearest. "His wife said to him, 'Are you still holding on to your integrity? Curse God and die!' " (Job 2:9). Yet Job held fast. "He replied, 'You are talking like a foolish woman. Shall we accept good from God, and not trouble?' " (Job 2:10).

Job stayed the course. That's integrity. No matter what happens, you're obedient to God. You recognize His power, even when circumstances are crazy. You recognize that He's in control, even when you can't explain what's happening.

As a last punch, Job's three friends came to him and basically made the same statement as his wife. For several chapters they argue that if Job had had any integrity in the first place, all this bad stuff wouldn't have happened to him.

But Job resolutely defended himself: "I will never admit you are in the right; till I die, I will not deny my integrity," he said to his friends (Job 27:5). "Let God weigh me in honest scales and he will know that I am blameless—if my steps have turned from the path, if my heart has been led by my eyes, or if my hands have been defiled" (Job 31:5-7).

At the end of the book, Job is vindicated by God. God won the contest. And God rewarded Job for keeping his integrity. God made Job twice as prosperous as before. Job was blessed with hordes of new sheep, camels, oxen and donkeys. New children were born in his family. His daughters are described as the most beautiful in the land. Job lived a long life and saw his children and their children to the fourth generation.

That type of blessing is not specifically promised to us today. God doesn't vow that He'll give you a new car if you stay steadfast in what you know to be true. Sometimes your life can become even more difficult. It was that way for Job at first. But integrity is always the wisest path. The rewards of integrity still exist. Some are obvious. Some are more subtle.

Perhaps it's easier to see the rewards of integrity when you consider the alternative. What does it look like to be a person without integrity?

It's nobody you want to be.

GETTING PUNCHED
The Pledge You Only Think Is There

What does it look like when integrity is absent?

Another dating story:

In college, I (Shaun) was convinced that I had found the love of my life. We dated all through my sophomore year; then I took the plunge and popped the question. We were engaged through my junior and senior year.

It was serious. She had an engagement ring on her finger. We had slapped down a chunk of our money for her wedding dress. Our parents were involved in planning the big day. People were marking the date on their calendars. This wedding was on.

And she was a five-star woman. I totally loved her. Sometimes she traveled with me to weekend ministry gigs. Sometimes she couldn't make it, and that was okay—she had her own life to lead too. Every few weeks she'd travel to her home state to see old friends. I didn't think anything of it.

One day, a few weeks before the wedding, I was up in her apartment on campus for dinner, and the phone rang. A guy was on the other end. "Hello, is Matilda there?" the voice said. (Not her name, obviously, but that's what we'll call her.)

"Yeah," I said. "Can I tell her who's calling?"

Have you ever fielded one of those sudden blows—the kind when everything you've thought was true is zapped by a sucker punch? That's what happened to me in the next two seconds.

"This is her fiancé," said the voice on the phone. "Who's this?"

Matilda turned from the kitchen where she was getting dinner ready. She must have seen my face lose all color. "I can explain everything!" she said.

I hung up and stood there, beads of cold sweat on my forehead.

Her words jumbled out. The guy on the phone was an old boyfriend—she really cared about him, she had never totally severed things with him. So yeah, she was engaged to him as well as to me. Whenever she traveled out of state it was to see him. Whenever she saw him, she took off the engagement ring I had given her and put on the engagement ring from him. It was only so she could work things out in her head, she said. She just needed some time to make the choice between us. And she was sure at last.

"I've decided," she said. "And it's *you*."

Time? I wondered. We had been engaged for nearly two years.

"I've made a decision too," I said. I shook my head. "And it's *not* you."

She pulled off the ring I had given her and threw it at me.

I slammed the door behind me on my way out.

I remember going for a drive that night, having the same conversation with God that I had had when I was fired from the first church I worked at: "God, what's happening to me? I'm giving You my life, but the rug is being yanked out from under me. I just don't get it!"

Matilda's dad phoned two days later, trying to patch things up for us. "Let's get to the bottom of this," he said. "We've got a wedding to plan."

"We've got nothing to plan," I said flatly. I was finished. This girl had demonstrated what I believed to be a lack of integrity. She had deceived me, pretending to be devoted when she wasn't. It was no way to begin a marriage.

The next season of life was one of the hardest I've ever gone through. Nothing seemed the same. My studies suffered. I lost weight. My heart was broken. I was wrecked. Another challenge was before me: In the midst of my pain, would I crumble under the pressure? Would I maintain my own integrity? I could have drowned my sorrow in drunkenness or gone out and found some floozy to sleep with in an attempt to quell my pain. I could have harbored a grudge against my former fiancée, clutching anger in my heart.

Fortunately, I didn't. None of that would have done any good. Instead, I turned to the Lord. I was convinced that God had been faithful before, and He'd be faithful now—even in the midst of this dark night of the soul.

The end of the story? I never married Matilda. I mean her and her family no harm now, even in telling this story. But put simply, Matilda was nobody I wanted to spend the rest of my life with, not after I found out the truth. I think in my heart that I've forgiven her now, years later. I hope that she doesn't hate me.

In hindsight, everything worked out well. Last I heard, my former fiancée is happily married to someone else. And so am I. I would never have the wonderful wife and kids I have today unless that horrible season happened. God is able to redeem all things, no matter how painful they once seemed.

What else happens when integrity is absent?

The punches surrounding a lack of integrity emerge like this: Sometimes it's hard to know which path to take. It's hard to discern what's right and wrong, what's healthy and harmful. Discernment is hard work, and it takes time, prayer and emotional and mental energy to figure out what the truth is in a situation. It's so much easier just to go with the flow or follow the crowd, or assume that things are smooth even when they're not.

A punch comes in the form of temptation: After you've discerned what is truth, you're tempted to not act on it. Usually there's some sort of personal cost to your decision if you take the next step. You risk embarrassment. Or risk a cut in pay. Or risk looking like a goody-goody if you follow the path of integrity.

Still another punch comes from the temptation to weasel out of responsibility while desiring to appear squeaky clean. You want to look like you have integrity, but you don't really have it. This is when you announce that you're acting on your discernment, but then you don't actually do anything. Your actions are hypocritical—you have the appearance of doing the right thing but the practice of doing another.

No one ever said it's easy to have integrity. That's part of the challenge of becoming mature. When the punches of life come at you, you know what to do.

So how do you develop integrity? It might look different from the way you've imagined. It might even mean picking wheat on a Sabbath.

TRUE TOUGHNESS
Christ, Integrity and All the Stuff He Did the Wrong Way

What does it look like to develop true integrity?

At its core, integrity is a heart thing, not a behavior thing. Go to the Gospels—what do they say?

A group of ancient tighty-whities called the Pharisees prided themselves on keeping all the outward appearances of looking good. Their goal was to be men of integrity, but they believed that the means to that integrity was to follow a list of rules.

Bold-faced and blatant, Jesus Christ told them that they had the wrong focus. For instance, the Pharisees thought they had integrity when they kept the commandment to not commit adultery. For them, it was all the letter of the law. As long as they kept their pants on, every other action with a woman, any woman, was a go.

But Jesus turned their system on its head: "Anyone who looks at a woman lustfully has already committed adultery with her in his heart," Jesus said (Matt. 5:28). In other words, real integrity means that your heart is in the game, too, not just your pants.

In another instance, the Pharisees believed that if they prayed a lot, they were doing the right thing. So that meant praying as loudly as they could, outside where everybody could see them and notice what fine fellows they were. Again, their emphasis was on the action—the behavior—not the heart.

Jesus got to the core of the matter. If you want to truly pray, "go into your room, close the door and pray to your Father, who is unseen" (Matt. 6:6). The emphasis was inner integrity. Sincerity—an honest heart and the actions that resulted.

So what does this mean for us today?

As Christians, it can be so easy to let the quest to be right all the time drive the development of our integrity. We create lists of dos and don'ts that we try to maintain to stay solid. As long as we keep our list, we think everything will be okay. Similarly, if friends stray from our list, or create a different list, we conclude that they're blowing it, and we feel a need to chew them out or not associate with them, or whatever.

But Jesus' example of integrity was always about aligning the heart with what's noble, never about blindly following rules.

When I (Marcus) went to Bible college in the late 1980s, this latter type of tightrope integrity was sometimes pushed. The student handbook contained lists of morality guidelines, some archaic and outdated—such as, you had to wear a shirt with a collar to classes. Some people at college—not all—defined integrity as adhering to the student handbook at all cost.

For example, one of the resident assistants was invited to dinner at a professor's house where an elderly aunt of the professor's was staying. The aunt was a widow, and when the professor left to go to the store to get some ice cream for the dinner, the resident assistant found himself in a moral quandary—you see, it was against the school's rules for an unmarried guy to be alone in a house with an unmarried woman. It didn't matter if the woman was 85. Rules were being broken. So this poor guy excused himself from the living room where he was chatting politely with the elderly aunt and stood on the front porch in the rain until the professor returned.

When the story was told, a few administrators held this up to us as the epitome of integrity—that this poor shmuck cared so much about doing the right thing that he chose a ludicrous action for the sake of his character.

I don't question the guy's integrity. I question a system that created weirdness. Why wasn't there a clause built into the student handbook that allowed for flexibility when a situation called for it? I wonder if Jesus would have left the elderly aunt and stood on the porch.

Did Christ also check over His shoulder when He dialogued with the woman at the well? Or would Jesus have recognized a higher law at work and followed that instead—the law of loving God. Christ was never a rule breaker for the sake of indulgence, yet He often challenged rules when rules were stupid, pointless or flat out hurt people. For instance, in John 8, an adulterous woman was brought to Jesus. The law said to stone her—but Jesus raised her up from the dust and declared that she wasn't condemned. In another instance, Christ was walking through a grain field on a Sabbath, picking wheat. Rules said you weren't allowed to do that, but Jesus knew His disciples were hungry, and He picked the wheat anyway. A higher law was at work. Rules always must benefit people, never the other way around.

Real integrity is about following a person—Jesus Christ. His focus was about a relationship with the Father. When you follow Christ and His model of living, your life will be filled with true integrity. You'll do the right thing because you honor God, not because you're a rule follower.

It's this love for Christ that develops true integrity (see 2 Cor. 5:14). Paul says in Philippians 1:9 that the pathway to discernment is through prayer and love. Those are the two principles that must always guide our decisions.

So let's put this into practical terms. If integrity means doing the honorable thing—not because rules say so, but because of a relationship with God—what might that look like?

- Maybe a group of friends are out getting drunk on Saturday night. What will your actions be under the guiding principles of prayer and love? Mainly, your goal is to love God. How will that play out? Who knows? Perhaps you're the designated driver, or you stay home, or you hang out with a different group of friends, or you help lead them to a different activity or you come visit them in jail when they get arrested for drunk driving. Again, the focus of your integrity is not that you're a rule follower—it's that you love God.

• Or maybe you and your girlfriend are getting too close physically. What do you do under the guiding principles of prayer and love? Again, your goal is to love Christ. So perhaps you enlist a trusted accountability partner to help you set your boundaries, or you break up with the girlfriend, or you marry her, or at the very least stop touching underneath her sweater until you figure things out—again, not because you're a rule follower, but because you love God.

How do you develop integrity? You start facedown, as we talked about in the first chapter. When you love God, the rest of life comes into focus, including integrity. Integrity is the undergirding principle behind every facet of maturity. It's the steel that holds up the high-rise structure of your entire life.

And integrity is always a choice. We can't control many of the circumstances that come our way, but we can choose to love Christ in the midst of those circumstances.

That's what it looks like to develop real maturity.

DEVELOPING YOUR CODE
A Series of Decisions

Is it possible always to have an honorable heart?

Will you lose your integrity if your heart leans in a harmful direction, just once?

Good questions.

The focus of integrity is never that we try to whip ourselves into being super-Christians. We develop integrity because we ask the Lord for it, and also because we decide to go that direction by loving God. It's that same paradox of Christ at work in us and our will in action, working in tandem.

So, is it possible always to have an honorable heart? The Bible says that when we follow Christ, we are new creations (see 2 Cor. 5:17). The old has passed away. Yet the Bible also recognizes that there are sins that easily entangle us (see Heb. 12:1). It seems like a contradiction, but it actually fits together. Even if you find yourself in sin, you can turn around at any point and be an honorable man. Integrity is a series of decisions you continually make, rather than a quality you gain or lose in one fell swoop. But, yes, your life can be severely impacted by one bad decision. Some consequences are harder to bear than others.

There is no one set plan to follow that creates practical integrity in your life. That's why we're respecting you by letting you figure out your own code. Let's do some work right now. Success in the area of integrity means tailoring what you know to the specifics of your life. Work through these questions by yourself, with a small group of trusted guys, or one on one with a mentor:

1. What does it mean for a young man to have integrity? What are the benefits of integrity? What might it look like if a guy doesn't have it?

2. What are the areas right now where you struggle the most with integrity?

3. What steps do you need to take today (maybe every day) to ensure true maturity in this area?

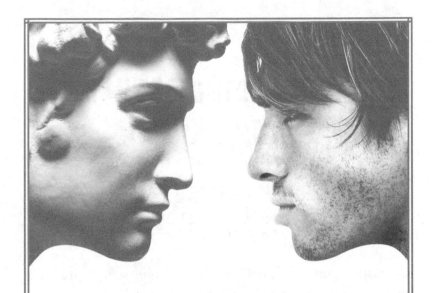

ONE THING TO THINK ABOUT:

INTEGRITY STARTS NOT BY FOLLOWING RULES, BUT BY FOLLOWING A PERSON— JESUS CHRIST.

DEVELOP YOUR CODE FROM HERE.

APPLAUDING ESTHER

THE CODE OF CHIVALRY

In Canada, where I (Marcus) grew up, we hardly applauded for anything. We cheered when the BC Lions won the Grey Cup, but that was it.

So imagine my surprise as a new high school graduate when I crossed the border to attend college in the States and found that people south of the 49th parallel clap quite a bit—after a lecture, after every worship song in chapel, standing around a TV on Sunday afternoons rooting for the Cowboys. We'd all just cheer away.

In graduate school, my applause meter was upped again when I traveled to Israel for a study tour. On the way over, we stopped in London for a long layover. Of first importance was food, so we headed to a buffet where everybody ate the same thing. With all the time zone mixings, our day and night had become switched. We were hungry for Cap'n Crunch and orange juice. Instead, we were served a heavy beef dinner with buttered carrots, Yorkshire pudding and roast potatoes in gravy. The noteworthy part of the meal came when the waiters brought dessert. They strode together into the dining room with a huge platter of cake on their shoulders—it looked like they were hefting a silk-enclosed litter with the Sultan of Sheba on it—and the entire room went nuts over the cake. Seriously—

all the locals clapped. I had never clapped for dessert before, but I could see why people might feel that way.

More clapping was just around the corner. Dinner consumed, we headed back to Heathrow airport and boarded another plane for Tel Aviv. When the plane landed, all the frequent fliers broke out in applause. I had never heard of cheering for a safe airplane landing. But it made sense.

So, what does all this talk about clapping have to do with a chapter on how to treat women?

It's this: Chivalry, at its foundation, means applause. If you don't normally applaud for women, don't worry. We're not encouraging you to toss a bag of Doritos over the women in your life. Real chivalry is a heart attitude of admiration—it begins in your thoughts, attitudes and motivations. If people all over the world can applaud for stuff like football games, dessert or airplane landings, then why not applaud for something as important as the opposite gender? It doesn't mean actually slapping your hands together whenever you see a girl. It's all about treating women with respect, praise, appreciation and acclaim. In a word—applause.

AS IT UNFOLDS

One of the challenges with chivalry is that it's not an idea we use much today. Maybe you've heard that it's dead. Or maybe you picture knights on horses rescuing damsels in distress. Or your idea of a chivalrous guy is some dude from the 1950s. He's got the fresh-faced charm of Archie Andrews, and he's polite to girls only because he fears that Veronica Lodge will slap his face for getting too fresh at Pop Tate's Soda Shoppe.

But real chivalry means that you root for someone's goals and ambitions. You cheer for what they find important. When it comes to the women in your life, chivalry means honoring their character, heart, achievements and whole person. Chivalry wraps around courtesy and consideration. It embraces courage and bravery. It requires valor and respect—all the character traits you want to develop in your journey to become a real man.

Chivalry was spurned not too long ago. It was made fun of, even crusaded against. How dare a man hold open a door for a woman?! This was the era of Gloria Steinem and bra burning—and not all of that was wrong, although the movement was highly controversial. The noble part of the feminist movement was that women fought to receive an equal voice. Justice was served. It was not good that women ever got paid less money for doing the same jobs as men, or weren't taken seriously in politics or the business world or were made to feel purposeless or powerless because of their gender.

To be clear—the goal of developing chivalry in your life today is not to return to the social roles of the pre-feminist movement. It's not about classifying women as a weaker sex, downgrading them to second-class or thinking they aren't capable of high achievement. On the contrary, chivalry is about honoring women, everywhere. Chivalry recognizes that women are different from men only because each gender is unique. But in skill and voice and strength and vision, chivalry recognizes that women and men are equal. If there are women reading this book, we hope you agree that being treated with honor is an okay thing. Hopefully, chivalry is in everybody's best interest, male or female. That's certainly the attitude by which we write this chapter.

So, back to our definition of chivalry: a heart attitude of applause for the opposite gender. Why might this be a good thing? Certainly it's an outworking of the Golden Rule—you treat other people the same way you want to be treated. If you're cool toward women, hopefully they'll be cool in return. But it goes further than that, because real chivalry doesn't expect to receive anything back. It's more about living with a purpose: Chivalry is part of the way you were designed to be. When you're chivalrous, you're modeling true love, selfless love, the kind of love God has for us. This is our call as men—to treat women as God intended, with honor, love and respect.

How do you develop this code?

Sometimes it means starting out the wrong way.

CHISELED TRAINING
Applauding Esther

If the idea of applauding women sounds foreign to you, don't worry. A lot of guys start out having no idea how to develop this code. Their stories are littered all through the Bible.

In Genesis 2:24, God says it's not good for a man to be alone. This statement forms the groundwork for chivalry. Adam is wandering around in the Garden of Eden with all he could ever ask for—but he's all by himself. And God says that sucks. That's an important first realization for guys—we need women in our life.

I (Shaun) can attest to this. My wife, Teresa, brings huge perspective to my life. If it wasn't for her, I'd be living in an empty box with one recliner and a big-screen TV. Guys are complete as single people, but we are much more when we are in community with women. The opposite gender brings the balance we need. This is the Bible's example to us from moment one.

Soon after Adam and Eve meet, things go haywire. The curse introduced confusion between guys and girls, and for the rest of the Bible, the confusion shows. Both Abraham and Isaac lied about their wives, saying that their wives were actually their sisters to protect themselves while putting their wives in danger. Moses' wife thought he was spineless. King David thought every woman he saw was his. It's true—guys can make a lot of mistakes along the way.

But chivalry does exist in the Bible. And some of the guys who started out as the biggest boo-ers of women made some of the largest strides in how they treated women later on. King Xerxes fit this profile. He was used to always getting his way. And why not? He was king of the world. What does a king do when he's got unlimited power? He throws a party. For a full six months, King Xerxes showed off everything he owned. At the end of the exhibit, Xerxes threw two week-long parties—one for the men, the other for the women. Picture it: In one huge banquet hall, there was King Xerxes with all his dudes doing chicken wings and beer. In another, Queen Vashti and the girls were doing Lee Press On Nails and Diet Coke.

Things at the guys' party got out of hand. King Xerxes, drunk, gave the command for Queen Vashti to come in to the men's party and parade around naked. The queen said no. All the guys were in an uproar about this. What would all the rest of the women in the kingdom think? There'd be no end to the household havoc. With his buddies egging him on, King Xerxes decreed that all women everywhere needed to obey their husbands. He also banished Queen Vashti from his presence forever. One problem—King Xerxes was now without a queen. And quality queens weren't that easy to come by.

So King Xerxes's buddies hatched a devious solution: a huge beauty contest. Scouts in search of hotties were commissioned to scour the land for virgins. If you had a finely featured sister, daughter, girlfriend—she was snatched up, no questions asked. The king's harem wasn't jail—the girls were treated well. But they couldn't leave, either. Once in the king's harem, the women stayed there the rest of their lives.

The contest rules were simple: After a year of beauty treatments, each virgin went to the king for one night. It wasn't for conversation or to test her brilliance; it wasn't about her character, personality or whether she knew anything about the queenly functions of ancient Persia. It was extremely intense and intimate. The king would marry the girl who pleased him the most. For the rest of the girls, life in the harem meant that they would never have husbands or families or occupations—or lives—of their own. Some might conceive and have children via the king, but that, too, was highly unlikely because most harem women only saw the king once or twice in their life. There were just so many of them. This contest showed the ultimate lack of respect for women. King Xerxes started out as the epitome of everything a real man isn't.

Fortunately, the story doesn't end that way. Over Xerxes's life, he became an applauder of women, not a boo-er. And it took a strong woman to show him the way.

It happened like this: A young Hebrew named Esther was caught in the virgin roundup and put in the king's harem. Esther went through her year of beauty treatments, waited in line for her night with the king, and was chosen as queen.

Some girls in her position might be content to live a life of luxury—to sit around and sip champagne all day. Esther initially appeared to have been tempted in this direction. When evil came her way, the type of evil a person is frightened to confront, Esther toyed with not doing anything about it. Her cousin Mordecai set her straight: "If you remain silent at this time, relief and deliverance for the Jews will arise from another place. . . . Who knows but that you have come to royal position for such a time as this?" (Esther 4:14).

The backstory is this: A meddler named Haman, who had been promoted to kingdom authority second only to the king, had tricked the king into signing an edict that guaranteed death for all the Hebrews in the kingdom. That meant death for the Jewish Queen Esther, too, which King Xerxes didn't initially realize when he signed the edict, because he didn't know she was a Jew. When Queen Esther found out about the plot, and with Mordecai's encouragement, she rose to the occasion. She fasted and prayed for wisdom, and then went to work on behalf of her people.

Reasoning with the king, particularly when the king was clearly wrong, was no easy matter. The queen couldn't just barge into the king's throne room and set him straight. To walk into the presence of the king unannounced meant instant death for anyone—even the queen. Only if the king was pleased to see you would your life be spared. So the queen put on her best duds, took a deep breath and went to see the king. Fortunately, the king was happy to see Esther. The queen played a careful poker hand, not tipping it too soon. She merely invited the king to a private banquet—a lavish meal just for the king and Haman. Xerxes was pleased at the first banquet, so Esther gave another banquet the following day, where she revealed Haman's horrible plot to kill all the Hebrews.

King Xerxes finally started to show some real character. Remember, he had a harem of women at his disposal. It would have been little problem for him to let Esther die with all the rest of the Jews. To be shown that he had signed a stupid edict was to be shown that he had used poor judgment. To admit that he had been duped was no easy matter for the king. He momentarily left the room in a rage, and when he came back, he saw Haman "falling on the couch where Esther was reclining" (Esther 7:8).

"Will [Haman] even molest the queen while she is with me in the house?" Xerxes asked in a fury (Esther 7:8b). That's a great line. It showed who the king truly valued—his wife.

The king made quick work of Haman and had him hanged on a gallows. Then the king issued another decree that said the Hebrews could arm themselves against any attack. In the end, the queen and her people were saved. What the end of the story showed about King Xerxes is that he grew to love Esther's mind, not just her body. He honored her and her intelligence. He trusted her and respected her more than Haman, a man, which was not common in that era. Xerxes came to Esther's protection and championed her cause.

Xerxes *applauded* Esther.

That's chivalry. Actions like that, and the heart behind those actions, are what we need to develop as young men.

But a lot of punches come our way.

GETTING PUNCHED
A Fury of Blows

It's not easy to be chivalrous. Childhood is all about self-absorption—we are not naturally chivalrous as kids. Chivalry is something we must learn in order to become men. But maybe your dad didn't model chivalry for you. Or maybe you don't know many men who fit this profile so that you can see how it's done. Certainly, you're not seeing much true chivalry on TV or in the movies. So what do you do?

Think about some of the beliefs, behaviors and attitudes that fall into the category of *not* applauding women. These are the childish ways that we want to put behind us as we become men. These are the temptations we want to resist and overcome in our lives. These are the punches that come at us fast.

The Punch of Lust

Lust can exhibit itself in a lot of different ways. Maybe you want to make out with every girl you see. Or you imagine her naked.

Sometimes a lot of lust emerges for a girl you've been dating for a while; sexual frustration sets in and you get impassioned for one thing only.

Lust can also be a problem when you're not dating anyone. Your life is a dry desert, and any drop of womanly water appears like an ocean of feminine possibilities. A girl says hello to you on the sidewalk and suddenly you're in bed with her in your mind.

Come to think of it, lust is *usually* a problem for guys.

How do you treat women with honor while grappling with that?

The Punch of Dating Ambition

Every girl you see, you view as a potential date. You might be drawn to a girl, but you just can't handle the possibility that she may never be more than a friend. You must get somewhere with her. Anytime you're around her you're ticking off the wish list of qualities you want in a potential girlfriend, or wife. You push too hard, too fast.

When I (Shaun) was in high school, one of my classmates won the Miss Teen USA pageant. She was perfect; she loved God, and she was hot—what more could a young guy ask for? I wanted to date her so bad. I called her all the time, always asking her out. And she always said no.

I pushed too hard and drove her away. It's easy to be too forceful in a relationship, particularly when you're first starting out. It's hard to give her the space she needs.

The Punch of Fear

Sure, it happens. Girls can be scary. Girls have the power to embarrass you, or reject you. A girl comes your way and you stutter all over yourself.

When I (Marcus) first started dating my wife, I actually found it hard to eat in her presence. She was so wonderful that she made me weak in the knees, and my stomach followed suit. It took awhile before I relaxed enough to be myself.

I know a lot of guys who struggle with fear when they're around girls. The question to ask is always, What's the worst thing that could happen? But even then, it's not always easy to overcome the punch of fear.

The Punch of Insecurity
This is when you try to impress girls with your swagger. My (Shaun's) son, Austin, is in fourth grade right now. Last year was all about cooties and staying away from girls. But this year he started to like girls. One of my volunteers has a daughter in fifth grade, a super-cute girl. We did a tailgate party, and this guy brought his daughter. My son was talking and acting differently. Every time we walked anywhere near to where she was, Austin would jump up and touch a door jamb or something. He thought he was being cool. I'm thinking, *Dude, who are you? Your voice is ten times lower than normal.*

It can happen at any age.

For several summers, I (Marcus) worked at a summer camp. One of my responsibilities was driving the ski boats. Off hours, all the drivers would go behind an island and practice wild boating maneuvers—sometimes behind the wheel, sometimes on skis or wakeboards.

One of the moves we developed was hanging off the swim step on the back of the boat while zipping along at full speed. Important: We've learned in recent years that the boat's exhaust bubbles up in the same spot. So you can suck in a lungful of poisonous carbon dioxide while doing this—or even pass out and drown. So don't be an idiot. (Back then, we didn't know any better.)

Anyway—when it was just the guys out in the boat, this move always seemed ultra cool. One day a college girl visited camp. I was really interested in her. She was a good skier, so we took her out in the boat. Just to show off, I hung off the swim step when the Mastercraft hurtled along about 45 MPH. In my mind, it was all about impressing her. It was a move of bravado, of action—all the things I thought she wanted in a guy. But when I came up for air, she just gave me a confused look. It conveyed that she thought I was the world's biggest two-year-old. We never had a second date.

Word to the wise: Girls are rarely impressed by the antics we think will electrify them.

The Punch of Dating to Play Around

Every dating relationship ends up one of two ways—you either break up or marry the girl. So why would you ever seriously date someone you wouldn't consider marrying? To have fun? There are a lot of emotionally simpler ways of having fun.

I (Shaun) dated a cheerleader once who was totally hot, but she didn't have very upstanding morals. My dad pulled me aside one day to ask me what the heck I was doing.

"Aw, Dad," I said. "We're never going to get married."

"Then what are you doing with her?" he said.

It was a great question.

The Punch of Passivity

I (Marcus) am mentoring a younger guy in my church right now who finally got engaged. The engagement is a good thing, because for so long he kept holding back with her. They were perfect together. He could see it; she could see it. Everybody else could see it. But he wasn't moving. And she certainly wasn't going to do the asking. It takes a lot of courage to take the plunge to marry, and one area in which this guy lacked drive was taking the initiative in the relationship. They'd go out on a date and she'd say, "Where are we going tonight?" And he'd say, "I dunno. Where do you want to go?" It's okay to welcome her opinion, but girls like it when guys have a plan.

It's easy to be passive in a relationship, particularly if you're at all insecure, which a lot of guys are. Once, I (Marcus) was dating a girl who lived a couple hours away from me, so it wasn't as if we saw each other every day. I was head over heels for her, maybe too much so. A few months into the relationship she confessed to me that she had kissed another guy while we were dating. I so wanted this girl to love me that I was overly nice in the situation. "Oh, that's okay," I said. "Everyone makes mistakes." I just pretended everything was okay, but inside I was fuming. I chose the emotionally passive way out.

The Goofball Punch

Whenever you're around women, you're obnoxious, gross or an idiot. Sometimes guys can be like this. Whatever the reason, we choose to be goofballs. Or we treat them like they're a bunch of guys. Whatever happened to changing your socks before you go out on a date? I (Marcus) knew a guy in college who always dressed like a complete slob. Once I asked him about it. "Whoever ends up marrying me will have to love me no matter what," he said. "This is just the way I am."

Whatever.

The Punch of Preoccupation

A while back, we had a guy on our youth staff that I (Shaun) had to let go. The reason? Basically, when it came to women, this guy was a knucklehead. He wasn't showing signs of growing up either, and I didn't want his negative influence on students he was supposed to be leading the right way.

This guy was a huge football fan of a specific team (let's say it was the Atlanta Falcons). His wife was going to have a baby soon, and she was about a week overdue, but he had tickets to watch the Falcons play when they came to town. His statement: "This kid better not come next week, because I've got tickets to the game. I'm not missing it for nothing."

It would have been one thing if the guy was joking, so I asked him if he was. Nope. He was serious. In the continuum of importance, watching the Falcons ranked above his wife and newborn kid.

That's not chivalry.

I had another guy on my staff a few years back whose wife described herself as a Tetris-widow. Anytime her husband played the video game, she didn't see him for hours. I'm thinking, games are okay—but there's got to be a balance.

Again, not chivalry.

As a young husband, I tried to focus on the question, *How can I demonstrate love to my wife?* I didn't always succeed, but I always aimed in that direction. When our kids, Austin and Alyssa, were born, there wasn't a lot I could do at first. But if a baby was crying in the middle of the night, I'd open an eye and ask my wife how I could help. That's an act of chivalry. It's saying, I love my wife, so I'm willing to sacrifice . . .

a little time
a little sleep
a little Xbox

Whatever it is, I'm willing.

Are you ready for that? Because chivalry isn't always easy. When you develop the code of chivalry, your life won't stay the same.

TRUE TOUGHNESS
Mothers, Sisters, Wives

How do you develop the code of chivalry?

Maybe you know someone who models it for you. It's as simple as watching what that person does, then learning the heart attitude of applause in your own life. Often, that's the best way to learn something.

I (Shaun) want my daughter, who's seven now, to grow up knowing what it's like to be around a real man. I don't want her to waste her time wondering what guy is the right guy for her. I want to instill in her a picture of how she should be treated, her whole life. I see girls in youth ministry all the time who don't have this and are looking for it with other guys.

So each Saturday morning, Alyssa and I have a date. We've been doing it faithfully for the past two years, since she was five. Her favorite place is Bagels and Brew, a breakfast and lunch place. Her favorite breakfast is bacon, egg and cheese on a bagel, plus chocolate milk. My stupid body is lactose intolerant, so I get glop on a wheat bagel. But I don't care—if she loves the restaurant, we're going. The experience is all about applauding her.

In fact, I treat the whole experience as if it's what a real date will be like for her someday. I open the door for her. I'm not crude or gross in her presence. I speak kindly to her. I pick up the check. I'm constantly asking myself what kinds of things show her respect. What will she enjoy doing? The experience is all about honoring her.

So we'll go to the mall and look at earrings. Or I'll take her shoe shopping. We've gone to a movie she really wanted to see—*Ice Princess*, a film that she loved but I barely tolerated. We ate popcorn and held hands.

What do you do if you've never had chivalry modeled for you? The Bible is the place to go for wisdom. And the Bible is surprisingly straightforward on how to treat women. It just gives three main directives: two are found in 1 Timothy 5:2—treat older women with respect, and treat younger women as sisters. The third is found in Ephesians 5:25 and repeated in Colossians 3:19—if you're married, or heading that way, love your wife.

Let's look at those three directives more closely.

Chivalry doesn't extend simply to the girl you're dating. Chivalry is a code you extend to every woman you know—your mother, your grandmother, your sister, your daughter, your female professor or boss.

So what does it mean to treat an older woman with respect? It's the opposite of this: Once when I (Marcus) was in youth ministry, I was hanging out in the kitchen of one of my high school students. His mom was there, and two of his sisters. Everyone was just bantering stuff around when the high school guy went a bit too far and starting calling his mother stupid.

She looked a bit shocked. I looked a bit shocked. It wasn't my house, so I didn't feel that it was right to reprimand the guy where I wasn't the head of the household. The mother probably didn't want to embarrass her son in front of his youth pastor. I should have pulled the guy aside later on and called him on his behavior. But here it is now, in black and white . . .

NEVER CALL YOUR MOTHER STUPID.

Treating an older woman like you would treat your mother means that you value her wisdom. You value her care. Or maybe she simply needs your compassion. Maybe she isn't wise and doesn't care for you much. Or perhaps she's old and invalid, or tired and cranky. When you treat an older woman with chivalry, you respect why she is the way she is. Maybe she's 85, and you volunteer to drive her home from church. Or maybe she's your boss, and being chivalrous toward her simply means giving her the benefit of the doubt. Or maybe she's your professor, and respecting her means valuing her education and teaching experience. Maybe she's the lady behind the cash register, and chivalry is as simple as smiling, giving her the correct change and asking about her day.

How about the second directive—treat younger women as sisters, with absolute purity? What might that mean?

My (Shaun's) sister Shannon is three years younger than I am. I don't know if we were exceptionally close while growing up, but we're becoming closer and closer the older we get. Sure, I teased her when we were kids, but hopefully there was also brotherly protection going on, and support and encouragement, and even fun. That's what it means to have a sister. I'd do anything for her today.

Treating a younger woman as a sister doesn't mean that you could never date her. But it does mean treating her, and any other younger woman, with the same amount of respect as you would a member of your family. You might joke around with your sister, but if someone truly threatened her in any way, chances are you'd put on the gloves and start swinging.

How do you treat your sister? In a word, you care about her. That's the place where all chivalry starts.

The third directive is to love your wife. Love covers it all. What's the most loving thing you can do for your wife? (Or your future wife?) Let that question guide your actions. How will you treat the woman you someday marry? Scripture has a lot to say about love. First Corinthians 13 is the place to start: Love is patient. Love is kind. Are you being those things to a woman? That's chivalry.

DEVELOPING YOUR CODE
Both Sides of the Road

The code of chivalry is not something you develop overnight, but on the way to becoming a man. It starts with the heart attitude of applauding women, and it takes a lifetime to develop fully.

The good news is that there is hope ahead. Both of us (Shaun and Marcus) have made our share of mistakes when it comes to women, but we've also done a few things right. To begin with, we're both in happy marriages today. Shaun and Teresa have been married for 12 years. Marcus and Mary Margaret have been married for 10. Of equal importance, we believe that we're learning the honorable way to treat all women everywhere. We've developed the code of chivalry—of ducking the punches of lust, fear, insecurity and all that, sometimes taking it on the chin; but we get up off the mat, stronger and wiser for our mistakes.

King Solomon made his share of mistakes with women. But sometimes he got it right too. In Proverbs, Solomon showed what true chivalry looks like. For example, Solomon encouraged young men to rejoice in the wives of their youth (see Prov. 5:18) and to not let lust rule their lives (see Prov. 7). He stated that a kindhearted woman was of more value than a financially ambitious man (see Prov. 11:16). He placed a higher value on female discretion than on outward appearances (see Prov. 11:22). He mandated respect for mothers (see Prov. 15:20), and (though the exact authorship of Proverbs 31 is disputable) Solomon offered a full summary of what it looks like to be a woman of noble character.

Take some time on your own to read the whole chapter of Proverbs 31. The woman Solomon describes there is well respected, highly capable, runs her own business, buys her own real estate, manages a household of multiple staff, is strong, competent, wise and has an eye for beauty. The image of the ideal woman provided by Solomon is a far cry from being a doormat, a second-class citizen or a promiscuous hussy.

Let's do some work right now in developing your code. Work through these questions by yourself, with a small group of trusted guys, or one on one with a mentor.

1. What does it mean for a young man to "applaud" women? Give some practical examples of what this might look like (or not look like).

2. What "punch" do you struggle with most when it comes to how you view or treat women?

3. Basically, chivalry boils down to three areas: treating older women as mothers, treating younger women as sisters, and loving your wife, or future wife. What steps do you need to take today (maybe every day) to ensure true maturity in this area?

ONE THING TO THINK ABOUT:

CHIVALRY IS A HEART ATTITUDE OF ADMIRATION— IN A WORD, APPLAUSE.

DEVELOP YOUR CODE FROM HERE.

BANDED

THE CODE OF SPIRITUAL ASSEMBLY

Fact: If you're a young man and attend church right now, chances are that in a year or two, you won't. For some reason, church and youth group connect with high school-aged guys, but college guys drop out.

The statistics are against you. A recent study showed that while as many as 80 percent of you attend church in your last years of high school, the number drops to 52 percent during your freshman year of college, and to 29 percent your junior year.[1] College guys just aren't involved.

Why?

Maybe there's more freedom in college. Your mom (or your youth pastor) isn't nagging you to go to church each week.

Maybe everybody just gets busier in college. (But maybe not, because a lot of high school guys are just as busy.)

Maybe you don't have easy access to a church while in college. You've got to take the bus or subway, or bum a ride from a friend with a car.

Maybe you're just plain lazy. It's a lot easier to sleep in on Sunday mornings. You were up partying the night before and you need some shut-eye before classes again on Monday.

Maybe the older you get, the more church seems irrelevant. You'd like to go, but nothing there seems geared to you.

Here's another fact: If you went to church as a high schooler but aren't attending now as a college guy, chances are good that in a few years you'll return. Statistics show that you'll sit church out for about a decade—from age 19 to 29, and then start going again in your early 30s.[2] It's just that gap in the middle that's a problem.

Why is this gap so lame? It means you'll pass through your most formative years as a young adult with your Christianity on the back burner. All the life-shaping decisions of that decade—to finish college or not, what career to pursue, where to live, whether to get married, who to marry, whether to have children, and many more crucial questions—will take place without the positive influence of spiritual assembly.

Why might you want to get plugged into a church in your college years? It's like Luke Skywalker is hanging out on the two-mooned planet of Tatooine, taking his first steps toward his destiny as a Jedi knight. He wants to be the world's best X-Wing fighter pilot, and he knows he needs to surround himself with the best training and guidance possible.

What are his options?

He could go crawl back under the covers at his aunt and uncle's shack on Tatooine.

He could go shoot some hoops with his buddies, C-3PO and R2-D2. A good time, sure, but he'll never take to the skies that way.

He could hang out for the next 10 years in the desert, hoping life will make sense on his own.

Or . . .

He could suit up, go to the planet Dagobah and learn from the best.

Dagobah, you'll remember, is the place where Yoda lives. If you've never seen *Star Wars* and don't know what we're talking about, um . . . WHERE HAVE YOU BEEN THE PAST 30 YEARS?!

And uh . . . please, just try to follow along, because there are a lot of similarities between a young man going to church and Luke Skywalker going to Dagobah.

CHISELED TRAINING
Church, the Murky Swamp Where Yoda Lives

Can you picture Dagobah? It's the harsh, murky, humid environment where the Jedi-Master Yoda was exiled. Luke flies his X-Wing there to learn from the master after Darth Vader and the Stormtroopers overrun the rebel alliance base on Hoth.

At first glance, Dagobah is not much fun. The planet is covered in gnarled trees and fetid swamps, kind of like church is awash in gnarled worship music debates and fetid committee meetings. In Dagobah, huge lagoons are home to fearsome snakes and swamp slugs.

What's fearsome at church? Ever glance at your watch every 30 seconds—about every time the minister says "and in conclusion . . ."—but you know he's got at least 20 more minutes of brimstone left in him? Dagobah is a world plagued with overgrown jungles, off-the-wall creatures and constant rain. Church is plagued with overgrown announcements, off-the-wall adolescents and constant unsolicited advice.

Few would ever come to such a place willingly.

Except Luke Skywalker.

Why?

Dagobah is the place that helps shape him into who he's meant to be. During his grueling training on Dagobah, Luke learns the ways of the Force. It's the place where he learns to lift his X-Wing fighter out of the swamp using just his mind. He learns how to effectively slash with his lightsaber. In a word, he learns the next step of becoming the man he needs to be.

That's church. It's for training. It's for service. It's to shape and mold you, even if it's sometimes like a swamp. But it's easy to miss that perspective Sunday by Sunday, when you just show up to sing songs and endure the sermon and hopefully catch the eye of the girl sitting next to you. I (Shaun) was like that for a lot of years. I didn't understand the importance of church until I was in my early 20s. My dad was a pastor, so I grew up at church. I think I was birthed on the second pew. Every time the church doors were open, we were there. We *had* to be there.

But one day it began to click. I knew that someday I wanted to be involved in a significant work for the Lord, so I knew that I needed to figure out the relevance of my faith, and I began asking what this thing called church is all about. If I wanted to be a fighter pilot someday (or the spiritual equivalent of that), I needed to be in a place that helped shape me into who I was meant to be. For me, that's how I began to develop the code of spiritual assembly.

The problem with church is that we expect it to be summer camp. Sometimes church is fun, but the Bible offers a different outlook of the purposes of church. There are other reasons for going than simply to have a good time. It's a little like college. Is college always fun? Not exactly—it's needed, it's useful and it fulfills a need. But no, it's not always fun. King Solomon hints at the importance of such a perspective in Proverbs 23:12 when he states: "Apply your heart to instruction and your ears to words of knowledge."

What might be other purposes for church? To begin with, the Bible says that church is a place to band together with other spiritually minded people—even people with personalities that aren't exactly like yours. Why? Because there's something good that happens from not being by yourself all the time, particularly in a spiritual sense. Other people help us grow. We help shape them and they help shape us. Even when it's uncomfortable. Other people help us learn how the world operates. We become wiser with other people in our life.

Solomon recognized this. In Ecclesiastes 4:9-11, he mentions how important other people are: "Two are better than one, because they have a good return for their work: If one falls down, his friend can help him up. But pity the man who falls and has no one to help him up!" The apostle Paul also talks about the importance of this in Romans 1:12. When we see each other, it's to make each other spiritually strong, he says. We get encouragement from each other's faith.

Probably the most important thing to realize about church is that church isn't a *place* at all—so this is where the illustration of going to Dagobah breaks down a bit. Church is actually an entity. It's a living organism. It's not a building with siding, neatly trimmed grass and a steeple on the roof. We always talk about going to church, about attending church, about the pros and cons of a good church service. But really, church is us. Church is the gathering of all believers everywhere.

We don't *go* to church.

We *are* the church.

How do we know this? In 1 Corinthians 12, the apostle Paul likens church to a body where Jesus Christ is the body's head. Each person who follows Christ is a different part of the body, and each person has a different function, just like the various parts of a body have different functions. Some people are legs— they travel fast and hold things up. Some people are voices— they're mouthpieces for all that needs to be said. Some people are even like the colon—kind of gross, but needed, because it gets rid of all the crap. Each part of the body is important. No one part can tell another part that it needs to take a hike. That's us—the church—a body of believers all functioning together as one.

Paul continues this metaphor in Ephesians 4:12. The main purpose of the church is so that the body, God's people, can be "prepared for works of service." The service is so that everybody is built up, unified in the faith and spiritually mature.

When you gather with other people as the church, you're being given the opportunity to be built up. You're learning how to be an X-Wing fighter pilot, in a spiritual sense. In other words, if you're not gathering together regularly with a group of people for the purposes of spiritual formation, you're missing out.

There's one more verse that lays out the importance of regular spiritual assembly. This verse says that church is important, even through the college years. It's there in black and white:

> Let us not give up meeting together, as some are in the habit of doing (Heb. 10:25).

There's no way around it. We challenge you, and every other young man in college, to write that verse out. Tape it to the bathroom mirror.

Regular spiritual assembly needs to be part of your life.

GETTING PUNCHED
Dude, Where's My Coffee?

Still, it can be a drag to go to church. How do you deal with that?

Here's what can happen.

There you are on a Sunday morning. You're in your dorm room at college and it's 10:30 A.M., and your dorm mate has just whopped you over the head with a pillow and grunted, "Dude, we're going to be late again."

So you throw on the jeans you wore last night, stick on a hat, gargle some Listerine (for the chicks you hope you'll run into) and throw the Scion into high gear to make it to church five minutes late.

There is no college group at your church. Or if there is, you've missed it because it started at 10:00 A.M. So you grab a coffee at the welcome center and slip into a back row in the auditorium. Everybody is standing with their hands up, singing Barry Manilow songs to God.

Jesus, you take me out of this place.
Jesus, I just want to kiss your face,
Jesus, you're the true Gate,
Oh Jesus, let's go on a date.
Jesus, hold me in your arms.
Jesus, keep me safe and warm.
Jesus, you'd never leave me, no never,
Because Jesus, you're the best boyfriend ever.

Seriously. Think about some of the words to today's popular worship songs. They approach Jesus with the language of romantic love—and the lyrics, if you think about them, are something you'd never ever sing (or say) to another man, Jesus notwithstanding.[3]

So you're uncomfortable during worship. Then comes the sermon, which feels geared toward your parents, or maybe like another college lecture, and your head is already swimming from the week's studying. Then the offering is passed, which you never contribute to because you're always broke. Then church is over and you try to meet some chicks on the way out, but they're all in the bathroom doing their hair and makeup because they want to look good for you. So you miss each other in passing.

In the end, you walk out the door without saying hello to anybody. Church is officially over. You went. You did your duty—and that's what it feels like. You clocked in and clocked out, and now you can go do what you really want to do—get a burger and fries for lunch.

Below are the common punches of going to church—the negative attitudes, beliefs and practices that come our way. See if any of them apply to your church-going experience.

- You don't know anybody there, so you don't like it.
- You don't relate to the music.
- The message doesn't speak to you or what you're going through.
- All the friends you regularly hang out with don't go to church.
- You don't like the people in your college group.
- There's no task for you to do there, so you feel un-needed; church is for your parents only.
- You wanted something from your church, but it didn't deliver, so you're miffed.
- Your pastor's an out-of-shape dweeb—not the type of guy who inspires you to be the man you want to be.
- Church is never any fun.
- You feel judged when you go to church—people don't like your hair, your tattoos or where you've been the night before.
- People at church always seem so critical.
- There are no hot chicks at church . . . the only girls who go to church are stuck-up prudes.
- Church just doesn't do anything for you, so why go?
- You've got better things to do on Sunday mornings.

Anything else?

College guys can find a million reasons for bailing on church. If you're truthful with yourself, you could probably agree with at least a few of those punches. It's a long list. Take your pick. But most, if not all, problems with church can be boiled down to one statement, and most of us have uttered this at least once in our life:

Church doesn't meet my needs.

Maybe you had a need to be spiritually fed, and you weren't. Or you had a need to meet someone cool, and you didn't. Or you had a need to sing worship songs you liked, and you sang sappy stuff from 20 years ago. Whatever—it all boils down to your needs not being met. The result is always the same in the end: You have no regular spiritual assembly in your life.

Is there any hope for you and church?

What if there's a different way of looking at all this? What if this other way acknowledges that church isn't always perfect? What if somehow, this other way realizes there is value in spiritual assembly even when all your needs aren't being met?

Here's how the other way shapes up. Instead of thinking of church as a place you go to get your needs met, think of church as a tribe you belong to that helps you meet God. A tribe is just a group of people, all united by some common cause. Both good and bad stuff happen in your tribe. Sometimes the tribe holds a meeting that leaves you walking out the door with a smile on your face. Sometimes when the tribe gathers, it's a murky marsh with swamp slugs. But always, the goal of the tribe—it's your goal too, because you're part of the tribe—is to become who you were meant to be: a worshiper and a minister—someone who loves God and cares about other people; someone who lives the most extraordinary life possible, all because God works through him and in him; someone whose chief end and goal is to *enjoy* God forever.

What might happen then?

TRUE TOUGHNESS
The Tribe of Church

A few years ago, when I (Shaun) was a youth pastor back in Indiana, one of the guys on my youth staff was a 350-pound New Yorker named George. That's his real name too. And when I first met George, I couldn't stand him. He had buzzed hair and wore these big old ugly glasses. He wasn't super tall—just big— and he had a mafia hit-man personality.

At first glance, George was the most abrasive guy I had ever met. If a parent picked up a kid from youth group 20 minutes late, George ripped into the parent: "Hey, why you late? Wassa mattah with youse?! Doncha care about your kid? Don't be late again!"

I couldn't believe it. Where was the tact? George could be in my face too. If he didn't like something, he'd tell me straight up. One day he stopped by my office and he wasn't smiling. I figured he was about ready to turn an Uzi on me. But instead, he slumped in a chair, put his face in his hands and began to cry. The story came out: One of the kids he mentored was really going through a rough time; the kid's parents were getting a divorce. George really cared for this kid. The kid was hurting. And George was hurting right along with the kid.

That day was the turning point in my friendship with George. I realized we had a common bond: caring for kids, even if we showed it in different ways. We were very different people, George and I, but we were in the same tribe. He became one of my best friends, emerging as a top-notch leader and someone I consistently relied on to get the job done. The point? You never know who'll become your friend at church.

Story number two.

During my (Marcus's) first year of graduate school, I went to a college group at a church near the university I attended. I had just moved to Los Angeles and knew nobody. I rented a room in a house where just one other guy lived—a 72-year-old man who had recently lost his wife to cancer. Basically, I went to school, worked part-time as a waiter, studied, talked with the old man, and spent the rest of my time trying to meet girls. That first semester was pretty lonely.

When it came time for Christmas break, my plans were to fly home to see my folks. The problem was that I didn't know anyone well enough to ask them to drive me to the airport—Los Angeles International was about an hour (without traffic) from where I lived. So I phoned up the college pastor at my church, hoping he'd volunteer to give me a ride. Instead, he pointed me to a shuttle system. Honestly, I felt a bit miffed. Aren't pastors supposed to take care of the people in their group?

The funny thing was that my college pastor actually did me a much greater favor. He could have dropped everything on his busy plate to give me a ride, but instead he gave me the gift of independence. He respected me enough to know that I was old enough and smart enough to figure out the Los Angeles Airport shuttle systems on my own. In the coming years, I needed a ton of rides to and from the airport, and instead of going to my pastor each time, I had the maturity and skills to be responsible for myself. The shuttle system was much easier in the end, and it gave me a greater sense of adulthood and pride.

That's this crazy tribe called church for you.

Problems come when we expect to get along with everybody in this tribe, or when we demand that church meet all our needs. The reality is that this tribe is filled with the Georges of the world, people you might not necessarily get along with at first, and pastors (and other people at church) who seldom do what you want them to. Their job is not to please you.

When we start looking at church as a gathering of people we belong to that helps us meet God, it's only then that church starts to make sense.

Use this new model, and think of the people you know at church.

Chances are, there are a whole mix of folks at your church. Some are old, and some are young. Some are wacky. Some are cool. Why would you possibly want to gather with people so different from you?

Maybe—just maybe—your tribe works best that way. Think of church as a crazy family reunion; not everyone is your age, nor should they be. A family reunion is a big glop of folks. There are the wise grandparents, the wild seafaring uncles, the freckle-faced cousins, the drooling babies. Something good happens when you learn to get along with people who aren't exactly like you.

For instance, one of my (Marcus's) best friends as a high school kid was a 93-year-old woman everyone called Grandma Blanche. She was part of my tribe. Grandma Blanche had been married three times and outlived all her husbands, but she never had any kids of her own. So she just adopted everyone she met as hers.

At her funeral, person after person took the microphone and told stories about how Grandma Blanche had written them a note at just the right time, or stopped them in the foyer to say she was praying for them, or baked them cookies, or given them a little gift, or listened when they needed to talk, or whatever—the list of people Grandma Blanche's life touched went forever. I would never have had the privilege of knowing her unless I opened myself up to the possibility of friendships with people who are different from me. If you open your heart to the possibilities, you never know who's going to become your friend at church.

Another question: How do you deal with all the stuff that happens at church? What do you do if you don't like something? Use this new model:

Just last week, I (Shaun) attended church here at Saddleback and found myself hating one of the worship songs we were singing that morning. Saddleback is considered one of the best churches in the country, and I love it, but the point is that even at one of the most cutting-edge churches around, you are bound to find something you don't like.

So there we were, and I was hating the song, and everybody around me was worshiping standing up, and I just felt like sitting down.

Here's where some of the greatest opportunities in our tribe come to us—surprisingly, when our needs aren't being met. I could have walked out. I could even have quit my job and looked for another church. I could have tried to buck up and force myself to like the song. But instead, what if I had simply started praying?

I mean, really praying. Picture it: I'm standing in church singing a song I can't stand, and I'm telling God what's truly on my heart. "God, I hate this song. God, I just want to sit down and fold my arms. God, why do I hate this song? Because it feels old and dull, and I know that You're not that way. And I want people everywhere to know how great You are—and You're nothing like this song."

Suddenly, I'm having a true conversation with God. He's big enough to handle anything I can throw at him, even my unhappy attitudes. As I meet with God, He'll show me how I need to respond. Worship is never just about singing songs; it's about our hearts connecting with God. And even if we don't like a worship song, we can still connect with God in the middle of that song. We can still see God for who He truly is.

One last thought: True toughness is developed when we don't simply hang out in our tribe, but when we serve as a representative of our tribe. Church is all about being Christ's body in the world.

It can be so easy to just show up at church and think that everything should cater to us. But remember, we are the church. We are the tribe. If church feels miserable, or if church is boring, maybe it's our responsibility to help out. One of the most courageous things any man can do is volunteer to teach a class of junior high kids. And not just play games with them either. Face it—their skulls are mostly full of mush and hormones. What would it be like to really dig into the Word of God with them? To really show them what following Christ is all about? That certainly wouldn't be boring.

The point is not that we all need to teach junior high Sunday School; it's that we open ourselves up to whatever place of service God has for us. Our tribe is not simply a place we attend—we are the church, and our call is to serve.

Service does not happen only within the doors of a church building, either. Maybe God wants you to serve in a soup kitchen or volunteer at a hospital or join a mechanic's ministry helping low-income folks maintain their cars. Or maybe there's a single mother in your apartment complex—you just buy a box of diapers and leave it anonymously in front of her door.

Our tribe is the hands and feet of Christ in the world. We are the body. This is our church. Our church is us.

DEVELOPING YOUR CODE
You Belong Here

A while ago, I (Shaun) was talking to a lady I met at one of my kids' school functions. She asked me what I did for a living. I told her I was one of the pastors at Saddleback. Her line:

"Oh, we used to go to Saddleback, but we don't go there anymore. We realized the messages were just for sinners."

I'm thinking, *Aren't we all?*

The woman's statement pretty much sums up every attitude you *don't* want to have about church—that church is a place for other people, not you.

The truth is that church is for you. This is your tribe. It becomes part of what you make it. And everything changes when you go to church with an attitude of openness—*What do You have for me today, Lord? Where do You want me to help out? What role in this tribe do You want me to fill?*

This is the start of developing your code of spiritual assembly. It's what's needed to become a man.

Some practical things to remember:

- Your call is to belong to your tribe. It's not just to attend, but to serve.

- Make sure your heart is prepared when joining up with your tribe each time you meet. It's not about getting your needs met. It's about connecting with God.

- Realize that a church is not going to be a perfect place. It's made up of imperfect people, just like you. God uses people to help shape you to become who you need to be.

- You can connect with God even when things are hard at your tribe. Just start telling God what's really happening inside you. God is big enough to handle anything you throw at Him.

Let's do some work right now in developing your code. Work through these questions by yourself, with a small group of trusted guys, or one on one with a mentor.

1. Why is it important that you connect with a church?

2. The next time you're at church, and you find your-self not liking something there, what might you do about it?

3. What type of service do you sense you are called to?

Notes

1. Ed Vitagliano, "A Strange Faith—Are Church-Going Kids Christian?" November 15, 2005. http://headlines.agapepress.org/archive/11/152005a.asp (accessed September 2007). Vitagliono quotes from a 2004 study released by the Higher Education Research Institute at UCLA. See the full study at: http://www.spiri tuality.ucla.edu/results/index.html.

2. "Twentysomethings Struggle to Find Their Place in Christian Churches," the Barna Group, September 24, 2003, http://www.barna.org/FlexPage.aspx?Page= BarnaUpdate&BarnaUpdateID=149 (accessed September 2007).

3. For a bigger picture of why church is sometimes hard for you as a young man, read David Murrow's excellent book *Why Men Hate Going to Church* (Nashville, TN: Nelson Books, 2005).

ONE THING TO THINK ABOUT:

YOU DON'T GO TO CHURCH.
YOU ARE THE CHURCH.

DEVELOP YOUR CODE FROM HERE.

QUEUED

THE CODE OF A STRONG WORK ETHIC

It used to be that the customer was always right.

These days it seems that the customer's just an annoyance.

So the other day, I'm (Shaun) heading through the drive-thru at the Golden Arches, and I ask for a Big Mac without cheese because of my lactose intolerance. The kid hands me the bag at the window, I pull out of the parking lot, and I'm 200 feet down the road before I realize I didn't get what I asked for. This burger has cheese. Here's my dilemma: I could wolf down the burger and have a gut ache for the rest of the day. Or I could circle back through the drive-thru and politely request what I asked for.

I chose the latter. Word for word, my conversation went like this:

> **Me:** Hey man, sorry to bother you, but I ordered a Big Mac without cheese.
> **The dude (very flatly):** No, you didn't.
> **Me:** Actually, I did; I've got the receipt right here. It says "Big Mac w/o cheese."
> **The dude:** Nah, that's impossible.

How can I compete with that? Fortunately, a manager came to the window and produced a new Big Mac—minus the cheese this time.

But the first dude's response got me to thinking about what it means to have (or not have) a strong work ethic. I know that a strong work ethic exists. I've seen it in other guys his age. When people don't have it, life is much harder for everybody— even for the dude in the drive-thru window (though he might not realize it).

Why?

When you work haphazardly, or lackadaisically or with a surly attitude, you rob yourself of life's good stuff: the ability to work as God intended. Having a strong work ethic means being professional, diligent in your work and a team player with the people around you. But it's more than that. God knows that whenever you take what He's given you and use it for good, you benefit. He delights whenever you delight in the talents and abilities you've been given. God and work and being a man are closely intertwined. So when you work, you actually reflect something of the way God made you.

Think of it this way: One of the first things God revealed about Himself in the Bible was His capacity to work. "In the beginning, God created the heavens and the earth" (Gen. 1:1). That was a whole pile of work. And as soon as God created Adam, the first man, God let him experience what work felt like. God set Adam in the Garden of Eden "to work it and take care of it" (Gen. 2:15). So that's why the dude in the drive-thru window actually hurts himself whenever he pulls an attitude with his customers. He's being a cranky employee, yes, and no-body likes that. But the greater problem is that he's missing out on living intentionally. His apparent disgust for his work is not a reflection of the type of man God intended him to be.

Developing a strong work ethic is easier said than done. Why might the drive-thru window guy have such a surly atti-tude? Who knows? Maybe his grandmother just died, and he's legitimately hurting. Or maybe he's got a rock in his shoe. Or his collar's too tight. But maybe he's simply wrestling with the angst a lot of us experience when we don't have our dream job. He feels like he's waiting in a long line with no end in sight. He's sure he's doomed to work the drive-thru for the rest of his life. He hasn't seen yet how this job—even a job that's not ideal—will become part of God's plan for his life.

If you haven't already experienced angst with a job, probably you will soon. What's your dream job? Doctor? Tugboat captain? Youth pastor? Writer? Professional snowboarder? Pizza tester? Drummer in a rock 'n' roll band? You'll probably have a lot of jobs along the way before you land your dream job. And when and if you land your dream job, you'll be the low man on the totem pole for quite a while, no matter what company or industry you're in. And the possibility has to be faced: You might not *ever* land your dream job—maybe you'll always work at a job that you're not passionate about.

So how do you have a strong work ethic at a job you don't always like?

At a job that seems meaningless?

When you're paid dirt?

When your job feels like only a stepping-stone to something else?

Part of the answer means avoiding the bleachers. It's a piece of the puzzle in developing this code for yourself.

CHISELED TRAINING
Off-season at the Ballpark

Imagine you're the coach of a heavy-hitting baseball team.

It's the end of the season and you have three players with the potential to rack up the runs next spring. All three are capable, though they show different specific skills. At the end of the season, you give them some good coachly directives for the off-season: *Okay, guys, between here and there, I want you to work on X, Y and Z.*

Just suppose this is what happens: The first guy hits the weight room every day. He runs laps to develop his wind. He practices sprints to hone his speed. He fills up on skinless chicken, spinach, wholegrain breads and power shakes. By the time the new season rolls around, this guy's in top shape. The new season's practice sessions don't drain him, and he's whacking fly balls out of the park right and left.

The second guy works with weights all summer, but he doesn't log any treadmill time. He eats his share of skinless chicken but still enjoys regular sessions of donuts and ice cream. By the start of the new season, he's got power but no air. He can hit it between the right and center fielders, but he's gasping like a weed blower in reverse by the time he rounds second.

The third guy spends all his off-season on the couch watching reruns of *Friends*. He fills up on Twinkies and Ding Dongs. He doesn't run. He doesn't even walk. The heaviest thing he lifts is a six-pack of Mr. Pibb off the counter at Quickie Mart.

When he shows up to practice, he's got the power and strength of a second-grade girl.

How do you, as coach, respond?

To the first guy—*You've made first string.*

To the second guy—*You're on the team, but you'll start on the bench.*

To the third guy—*You're off the team, lardboy. If you want to be involved in baseball this season, find a nice spot in the bleachers.*

Stay out of the bleachers. It's part of the code for developing a strong work ethic. And how do you do that? You make the decision to work well. And with the help of Christ in your life, your heart has added power toward that direction.

Jesus told a story similar to the baseball analogy. Actually, it's the one from which the baseball analogy was built. It starts in Luke 19:11, and it's called the parable of the talents. It goes like this:

A king gives responsibilities to three servants, and then travels to a distant country to take care of other business. The first and second servants invest their talents (currency) to the best of their ability. But the third servant digs a hole in the ground and buries what he's been given.

When the king returns, the first two servants are rewarded accordingly. But the third is cast out of the king's presence. In a manner of speaking, he's sent to the bleachers.

The point of the parable of the talents is that everyone has different abilities and gifts. God asks you to use what you've been given. Work well and live well no matter where you are, even if it's the off-season, or you only have one talent. That's having a strong work ethic.

The story of Joseph is another example of this principle in action. Read the whole narrative in Genesis 37–50.

Joseph's a smart dude. Even at age 17, he's showing a real knack for leadership. But he's his pop's favorite, and this causes problems. Daddy gives him a special coat of many colors, and Joseph's 11 brothers are jealous; so 10 of them sell Joseph to some camel traders. Joseph is carted down to Egypt as a slave. While taking care of his master's house one day, Joseph is propositioned by his boss's sex-hungry wife. Joseph refuses her guiles, and she falsely accuses him of getting fresh with her. So he's thrown in the clink. In the end, Joseph's résumé as a young man includes slave and prisoner—not exactly dream jobs.

But here's the cool thing: No matter what job Joseph works at, he always puts his heart into it. Even as a slave, the "Lord gave [Joseph] success in everything he did" (Gen. 39:3). As a prisoner, "the Lord was with him; he showed him kindness and granted him favor in the eyes of the prison warden" (Gen. 39:21). Joseph does such good work in prison that he rises to management level. "The warden paid no attention to anything under Joseph's care, because the LORD was with Joseph and gave him success in whatever he did" (Gen. 39:23).

That's a good picture of a strong work ethic—it's about doing your work for the Lord, no matter what work you're doing. Work—all work—is a reflection of God. This theme is repeated in Ephesians 6:7: "Serve wholeheartedly, as if you were serving the Lord, not men." And again in Colossians 3:23: "Whatever you do, work at it with all your heart, as working for the Lord, not for men." When you've developed and live a strong work ethic, it means that God is your ultimate boss. You report to Him. But more than that, as you work, you can sense your true purpose as God's creation. Work has a spiritual value. It allows you to understand more of God. Work allows you to be the man you were designed to be—even when the work is as a slave, a prisoner or a part-time worker for a job at minimum wage.

GETTING PUNCHED
In "The Queue"

In many ways, both of us (Shaun and Marcus) have really great jobs today. We're both grateful for this. Shaun is the high school pastor at Saddleback Church. Marcus is a full-time writer and editor in the book industry. People kill for these positions, but neither of these jobs is without its challenges. There are days when both of us, individually, would rather work some other job. It's fair to say that probably no one ever gets to the place where his job is completely cool all the time. Did you hear that?

Also, to get to these positions, it took a long time in what we call "The Queue." Think of The Queue as the place where all guys have to pay their dues. It's the long line of getting your education, figuring things out, doing stuff that's less than you hoped, getting paid less than what you think you deserve, making contacts, and learning and relearning the company ropes—all the stuff that goes into a career.

If I (Shaun) was to count all the jobs I've held prior to the position I have today, I'd have to say it's at least 25. Maybe more. Here are the high points.

As soon as I became a teenager, my parents stopped paying for most of my stuff. They figured I needed to learn responsibility. My dad was a pastor and never made much money. So I needed to get a job.

When I was 13, I landed a job as a bagger at Joe O'Malia's grocery store. Off hours I stocked shelves. Most days, I worked after school from 4:00 to 7:00 P.M. I used most of the money to go on youth ministry events.

The summer I was 16, I became a commercial painter. My folks bought me an old Lincoln LTD II, but it was my responsibility to pay for gas, maintenance and insurance. So all summer long, I was indoors, painting offices. All day I'd spray the stuff, then sand and scrape while breathing in fumes, and come out covered in paint.

The next summer, I poured concrete. It was probably my worst job ever. The very first day, we were laying a porch in back of somebody's house. We'd mix the concrete in front, then wheelbarrow it to the back. I had just scooped up a load and was hefting it to the back when the barrow hit a rock and went over. My boss hollered a blue streak. The concrete set up pretty quick. Me and another guy did our best to hose it down, picking the rocks and concrete out of the grass by hand, but I doubt if that lawn was ever the same.

When I went to college, I paid for school myself, using scholarships mostly. Throughout college, I always had a job.

The first year, I worked as a cashier at a Nike factory outlet store. We got discounts on clothing and shoes. Everybody there was pretty cool.

The summer of my freshman year, I worked as a porter for Premier Cruise Lines, carrying people's luggage. On the days I wasn't a porter, I operated a forklift, loading pallets of food. It was also a pretty fun job, although the hours were rough. We had to be there at six o'clock in the morning and often worked until seven o'clock at night.

After that I worked in a variety of youth ministries, up to the job I hold today at Saddleback.

I (Marcus) could point to a similar number of jobs along the way.

I mowed lawns for neighbors as a kid, then had a paper route from age 12 on. There were a couple of RV parks near my house, so summers I developed a business selling newspapers in the campgrounds. In high school, I was a counselor-in-training at a camp one summer, which meant a lot of washing dishes and mopping floors. It was hard work but a lot of fun.

The summer after I graduated high school, I worked construction. Me and another kid my age were the absolute grunts of the crew, the lowest of the low. We shoveled bricks, hauled lumber, picked up insulation—any mindless tasks that needed to be done around the job site. Fortunately, the pay was pretty good.

In college, I worked in a food stockroom. Doing inventory in the freezer was the worst. I'd wear every layer of clothes I had and still come out frozen as a Popsicle. I worked there only a semester, then I got another job as a janitor, which was where I worked for the rest of college. It was grubby work, especially cleaning bathrooms. But the upside was that it proved a good break from studying. I worked in downtown Portland: I'd go to these huge offices at night when no one else was around, lock myself in, turn up the music and vacuum the night away. For several summers during college, I worked at a camp, first as a counselor, then on leadership staff. It was heady stuff and a lot of fun, but it was seasonal work, so I was still in The Queue.

After college, I interned at a church for a year in their youth and music departments. It was cool, but all over the place in terms of responsibilities. Then I decided to take a year to figure things out, so I worked as a busboy at a swanky restaurant, and later as a waiter.

I started graduate school and worked as a waiter again, then got a job in youth ministry, where I stayed for six years. My first church was in rural Washington State. The kids there knew things about milking cows that I couldn't even imagine. After that, I helped start a church and worked there for about a year before everybody got mad at each other and things blew up.

I needed a job fast, because my wife and I had a mortgage by then. So I answered an ad in the newspaper to be a reporter. Writing was always something I hoped I could integrate into my life in some way. The job at the newspaper was supposed to be my transition job until I went back into pastoral ministry, but I ended up staying there five years. Along the way, I developed a career as a book writer and editor. I started working on books part-time, then the work grew to encompass my job at the newspaper. A few years back, I made the jump to full-time writer, which is what my work is today, and I love it.

When you look at those two lists, they're probably similar to most men's in the sense that by the time you finally do what you want to do, you've done a lot of other things along the way. That's life in The Queue. While there, it can be difficult to see the forest through the trees. When you're elbow deep in soap suds, washing dishes, or scrubbing gum off someone's desk while working as a janitor, you're pretty certain that what you're doing is not your dream job. You wonder if your work will always be what you don't want to do.

Try a little experiment with some of the men you know—maybe your dad or uncle or whoever—ask them to list all the jobs they've ever had. You're bound to hear some good stories of life in The Queue.

Below is only a sampling of some of the punches you can expect along the way. This list applies to part-time jobs. It also is what to expect for your first several jobs right out of college. It can be easy to graduate and expect a sweet gig. But even though you've worked hard at college, nobody will let you run the show just yet. When you turn up for your first job, you're a freshman again, only now it's a longer line and a steeper learning curve.

In your jobs, you can expect to

- **Work hard.** Washing dishes for eight hours straight isn't easy. Neither is taking 600 kids to camp when you're youth pastor at Saddleback. The point is that you need to know that no one ever hands you a paycheck for sitting around.

- **Make less money than you imagined.** When I (Marcus) got my first job as a youth pastor, the average youth pastor was making about $30,000 a year. My first salary started at $16,500. I took the job anyway. I didn't take it for money. I took it because the job was at a good church where I knew I'd learn a lot.

- **Work longer, later hours than you'd imagine.** Expect it. When I (Marcus) was a newspaper reporter, we'd frequently cover city council meetings that would run until 11:00 or 12:00 at night. When I worked as a waiter, sometimes we'd work double shifts—two full shifts in one day. On construction crew, sometimes things would get busy and we'd work 12 hours straight—5:00 in the morning to 5:30 at night. One morning, driving to work, I was so tired that I closed my eyes and drove into a ditch.

· **Not have your suggestions taken as seriously as you would like.** Do you think anybody would follow my (Shaun's) lead when it came to moving concrete? Or what about Joe O'Malia? He had been in the grocery store business a long time. If I thought I had a better idea for stacking up cans of tomato sauce, chances are he had thought of it a long time before.

· **Not have all the perks the senior employees at the company have.** More vacation days, better cubicles— maybe even a better uniform. When I (Marcus) worked as a busboy, I wore black pants, a white shirt and a tie. But all the waiters, who were a step up the scale, wore black vests. Man, I wanted one of those vests. Funny what can motivate you.

· **Work some tasks that are just plain drudgery.** And there are a ton of them out there. *A ton.* A friend of ours recently graduated with his finance degree and got a job for a brokerage firm. You'd think that would be a sweet gig. But what does he do all day? He pores through endless lists, cold-calling potential clients. It means eight solid hours a day of being told no. How's that for a fun time?

· **Not get along with all your coworkers.** We've all had doggish managers, gossipy co-workers, cranky secretaries and supervisors who were flat-out louts. Yep. People are people, no matter where you work.

· **Field jealousy.** Maybe someone is better (in some way) than you, or you're better than someone, and he doesn't like it. It happens.

· **Get fewer vacation days than you hoped, if any.** Most part-time jobs will not give you any vacation days. For full-time entry-level jobs, the offerings aren't much better. When you're in high school or college, you get Christmas and spring vacations, plus summers off, so it can be easy to get used to having breaks like that—even if you get a part-time job during those breaks. When I (Marcus) worked at the newspaper, we got 5 days of paid time off only after we had worked at the company for a full year. After 2 years, it rose to 10 days off. After 5 years, it rose to 15 days. We didn't get any sick days at all. If you were puking, you took one of your vacation days to do it.

· **Do the jobs nobody else wants to do.** A lot of work environments have a let's-send-the-new-guy-to-do-it attitude. You're seen as the rookie for quite a while.

· **Not know everything, and have others laugh at you.** At any job, you have to make your way in. I (Shaun) came to Saddleback with more than a decade of youth ministry under my belt, but I've definitely had to prove myself, even here. It's not like my co-workers laugh at me here, but the principle is that true trust is only developed over time—at any job.

· **Meet people who've been there a million years.** Happens everywhere you go. Sometimes these folks can be a good resource, but other times they're jaded and cynical, stuck in a job they hate but too entrenched to do something about it. Watch it when someone pulls you aside and says, "Let me tell you how it really is around here."

- **Be taken advantage of.** It can happen. Sometimes you can get dumped on simply because you're the new dude. You don't know the ropes yet, so you don't know the appropriate boundaries of your position.

So what do you do? How do you work at a "Queue" job like you're working for the Lord? How do you keep the perspective that to work well means to live well, that all work you do is a reflection of God?

TRUE TOUGHNESS
All the Jobs You'll Do

King Solomon had a lot to say about work. He could have chosen a life of luxury if he wanted. He was a king's son, raised in palaces. But he chose not to sit around. He acted as a judge, making wise rulings between people with conflicting interests (see 1 Kings 3:16-28). He worked as a teacher, giving instruction about birds and reptiles, plant life and fish (see 1 Kings 4:33). He entertained dignitaries and acted as a diplomat (see 1 Kings 10:1-13). He undertook huge building projects, including a massive temple and an even more amazing palace; he planted vineyards, gardens and parks; he constructed reservoirs and managed huge flocks and herds (see Eccles. 2:5-7). He devoted himself to the arts and "acquired men and women singers" (see Eccles. 2:8). Toward the end of his life, he managed the stables for huge numbers of war horses (see 1 Kings 11:26). Such was his work as a king.

Throughout the book of Proverbs, Solomon talked a lot about the practical wisdom of what it means to work for the Lord. He wrote that lazy people are soon poor, but hard workers get rich (see Prov. 10:4); that a hard worker has plenty of food, but a person who chases fantasies has no sense (see Prov. 12:11); that you can either work hard and become a leader or be lazy and become a slave (see Prov. 12:24); that wealth from get-rich-quick schemes quickly disappears, but wealth from hard work grows over time (see Prov. 13:11); that being hungry isn't bad, if it causes a drive in you (see Prov. 16:26); and much more.

So what does it mean to have true toughness in the area of work? What does it mean to develop a skillful approach to living in the area of work?

We want to give you two sets of practical guidelines for developing your code. The first are some parameters of what sort of job to look for. The second are some strategies to make it on the employment playground.

Here's the first. It's built off the acronym P.A.P.E.R. The principles are not given in the order of importance. Rather, think of them as five criteria for seeking a job.

When it comes to seeking a job, look for:

P: Provision. Like it or not, receiving a paycheck is a huge reason for working. That's not wrong at all. First Thessalonians 4:12 instructs people to work "so [they] won't be dependent on anybody." Will the job you take provide for your financial needs, whatever they are in a given season of your life?

A: Aptitude. Can you do this job, or can you learn it? If you don't know how to swim, don't look for a job as a lifeguard. You might want to be a fighter pilot, but if you wear glasses as thick as Coke bottles, it's not feasible to seek being a pilot as a career direction. At what school subjects do you excel? If you like math, then look for a job that uses those skills. Do you like golf? Work as a caddy. God has given you natural talents, abilities and preferences—consider all those factor in the jobs you seek.

P: Partnership. Even if you're single, this is still something to think about as you look for a career direction. As a guy, it's easy to think only of yourself when it comes to a job. But the older you get, you'll want to factor in what your wife thinks about a job situation. If you love a job and your wife hates it, or vice versa, it probably won't be a long-term fit. Also, with some jobs, it's virtually impossible to do the job well and have a family. For instance, a friend of ours works as a military contractor and is gone overseas for up to two years at a time—he's often forbidden to disclose his whereabouts or even to have contact back home. That makes it really tough to be a husband and father. So, when seeking a career, factor in the partnership equation. Will what you do allow you to be married and be around home enough to be a good father?

E: Excitement. Being passionate about a job is a good thing. You might not love everything about the job, but maybe you're excited about what you'll learn, or the opportunities it provides, or where it leads. If you absolutely hate a job, chances are it won't be a good fit for you long-term. Sometimes a job carries a level of excitement only for a season. That may be your nudge to seek something new.

R: Reason. Last, but perhaps most important, does this job matter? Does it affect people in a positive way? Does it lead people closer to Christ? Is God glorified by what you do? If you see your job as without purpose, it will be hard to sustain it over time. Sometimes people think they can only find purpose in their job if they're pastors or missionaries. But you can serve God anywhere, and with virtually any job. My (Shaun's) dentist cleans teeth all day, but she's got an amazing ministry in who she talks to and in how she conducts her business.

TWELVE STRATEGIES TO SURVIVE AND THRIVE IN YOUR FIRST REAL JOB

1. **Study your job description.** Make sure that you know what you signed on to do and not do. Don't be afraid to clarify your boundaries. If baby-sitting your boss's pet St. Bernard seems suspect to you, don't be afraid to ask your supervisor if that's what's actually expected.

2. **Expand your skill set.** If someone hired you, chances are he or she believed that you had the skills to get the job done. So be confident, step up to the plate and swing hard. At the same time, if you don't know something, it's okay to admit that you don't, or that you still need to learn something.

3. **Be humble.** No one likes a cocky rookie. Refrain from coming into a new job and telling everybody how they can do things better. Keep quiet, learn the

way things are done and choose your personal cru-
sades very carefully. Don't expect stardom overnight.
And don't criticize your company, your fellow employees or your boss. Even if you absolutely know
you're smarter than they are.

4. **Own up to mistakes**. Everybody makes them. It's
okay to do so, but take responsibility when you make
a mistake. Treat mistakes as opportunities to get wiser.

5. **Take time off**. Think sustainable pace—particularly
if your job is in an industry you're interested in long-
term. How can you do this job (or be in this industry)
a year from now, or 10 years from now? Don't be
afraid to really enjoy your weekends. You cannot
afford to not take a day off.

6. **Commit to time on**. At the same time, don't be
afraid to burn the midnight oil, particularly in your
early years.

7. **Keep learning**. New innovations are coming
down the pike at the speed of a mouse click.
Everyone constantly needs to rethink how they do
things and why. Attend seminars. Read books. Study
your craft. Get the degrees and certifications to stay
current.

8. **Expect drudgery.** Maybe that's not what you want
to hear, but almost every job has components to it
that will feel routine. Particularly after you've been
at a job for a while. A huge part of job success is
learning to keep at something for the long haul.

9. **Get to know everybody along the way.** And be respectful and considerate to everyone—even if he or she is the low dog in The Queue. Secretaries, junior associates, porters, doormen, valet parkers, busboys. Not only is it the cool thing to do, but in many industries, job turnover is high and people get promoted quickly. If you're nice to a junior associate, he may well be a senior associate soon. Things will go better for you if you were respectful of him when he was the low dog.

10. **Dress the part.** If your company's look is corporate casual, don't show up in either blue jeans or a suit.

11. **Don't surf the net on company time.** Yep.

12. **Never embarrass your boss.** Uh-huh.

DEVELOPING YOUR CODE
For the Crows

How will you develop your code for a strong work ethic? You'll probably have a lot of jobs along the way; some you'll like, some you'll hate. But all jobs will have a purpose. Even if you hate a job, you've learned that's one career direction you don't want to go.

When you're young, it can seem like you'll never get to where you want to be when it comes to a job. But at the very least, remember this principle . . . I (Shaun) call it the Crow Code. It goes like this.

My senior year of high school, I worked as a dishwasher at a Chinese restaurant called Mr. Ni's. The owner was a swell guy whose first name was Bo, so his full name was Bo Ni. (Say it out loud if you have to—very cool name.) I played football during the week, then worked weekends at Mr. Ni's. So it was all day Saturday, then after church on Sunday with my hands in suds.

Washing dishes is seldom fun, but in a Chinese restaurant you have all these sauces and stuff, so it can get even grosser. But the strangest part of the job was this—and this is no lie: One day these two cooks were hanging out back of the restaurant, and one dude spotted a crow flying by. So he whipped out a shotgun and blasted away. In no time flat, the crow was defeathered, sliced, diced and sizzling in a pot. The two dudes ate it right there, spitting shotgun shells out whenever they crunched on one. No joke.

What's the Crow Code?

It's that there is no great point to the story above. But even if a job is completely wacky, at the very least you'll have some funny stories to tell 20 years later.

In the meantime, let's do some work right now in developing your code for a strong work ethic. Work through these questions by yourself, with a small group of trusted guys, or one on one with a mentor.

1. What does it mean to have a strong work ethic?

2. What are some jobs you've done that you didn't like? How might those experiences have been good? Did you learn something? Did you accomplish something you're able to put on your résumé? What other benefits can you think of?

3. What type of job can you see yourself doing long-term? What sort of purpose do you think that job has?

ONE THING TO THINK ABOUT:

THERE'S PURPOSE
IN THE QUEUE.

DEVELOP YOUR CODE FROM HERE.

BANKED

THE CODE OF FINANCIAL RESPONSIBILITY

When my (Shaun's) wife was pregnant with our second child, we went through a 13-week course on finances offered by our church. The theme of the class was how to surrender everything to God—money, family, job, house, future—everything. So during the time we were in this class, we prayed to surrender things to God—to commit everything to Him. We were not to worry about stuff—we were to live as if everything belongs to Him.

When at last our daughter was born, our prayers were put to the test. At first, everything appeared fine. Alyssa was born by C-section. Doctors said everything looked healthy. For 24 hours all was great.

The next day, I was holding my daughter when she turned completely blue. She stopped breathing. I hope you never have to experience that horror. It's complete panic. This kid you've just sweated over for nine months is suddenly knocking on death's door, and you feel powerless to help her. A doctor was in the room and raced to get her breathing again.

An hour went by, everything looked fine again, and then suddenly our daughter went limp in my arms. She stopped breathing again. Again panic, terror, frustration, fear. A nurse was able to get her breathing this time.

Another hour ticked by. Again, everything looked normal. This time, a friend of ours was holding our daughter. Suddenly,

Alyssa turned blue again. This time there was no medical staff in the room. I grabbed my daughter and sprinted to the nurse's station down the hall. "Help my daughter! Help my daughter! She's not breathing! Help!" Basically, I just freaked out. They grabbed Alyssa from me and rushed her to the Neo-natal Intensive Care Unit (NICU) where they got her breathing again. She was hooked up to a spider web of tubes and monitors to figure out what was wrong. All the doctors said was "We'll call you when we get it figured out."

For three days, our daughter lay in the NICU. Doctors performed every test imaginable, including a scream-inducing spinal tap. At one point the doctor came to us and said, "Mr. and Mrs. Blakeney, we don't know what's wrong. We just want to prepare you that your daughter might not live."

Something breaks inside you when you hear earth-shattering news. My in-laws, my wife and I were in a hospital room when that news came. We held hands and started praying. God must have been working in my soul in ways I wasn't aware of, because my prayer was this: "God, we were just in this class where we told You everything we have is Yours. That includes our daughter. If You want to take her, take her. We surrender her life to You. We give her up to You right now." We were all bawling.

Exactly one minute after we said "Amen," the phone rang. It was the NICU ward. "Your daughter has made an immediate shift in health," said the nurse. "She's got the first good color she's had in days. It looks like she wants to eat."

We all started crying again, then ran down to the NICU. Teresa picked up our daughter, and she started eating, always a good sign with a newborn. Doctors and nurses all had sort of happy, bewildered looks on their faces. A few days later, we were able to take Alyssa home hooked up to a breathing monitor. She was supposed to be on it for six months. Medical staff took her off it three months early. Alyssa's never had breathing problems since she was born. She's 8 years old now and in perfect health. She's a champ in gymnastics. She runs, jumps, sings and shouts. You'd never know she once came so close to not making it.

What does that illustration have to do with money?

Simply that everything in your life belongs to God. It's all His. Whether it's your family, your friends, your finances or your future, if you clutch something, it's bound to get squished.

Only when you release what you have back to Him does life makes sense.

DIAMOND JAW TRAINING
God's Upside-down Economics

Jesus used some strong words on the subject of money. It's not that there's something intrinsically wrong with it; it's just that with money comes the temptation to use it for all sorts of evil. Money can color our judgment. It can shove us off track when getting it becomes our most important goal. Sometimes in that quest, you end up doing things you don't agree with. Or you end up in harmful places. Or you cater to people who have money but ignore people who don't have any. First Timothy 6:10 contains a tough warning: "For the love of money is a root of all kinds of evil. Some people, eager for money, have wandered from the faith and pierced themselves with many griefs." Money isn't wrong. But the love of it is. Do you love money? How would you know if you did?

Luke 12:13 tells the story of a man who fit this picture. A rich manager owns a farm that has produced a good crop. Money's rolling in and the wheat's really stacking up. The manager's biggest problem becomes where to store all his wealth. He utters these fateful lines:

This is what I'll do. I will tear down my barns and build bigger ones, and there I will store all my grain and goods. And I'll say to myself, "You have plenty of good things laid up for many years. Take life easy; eat, drink and be merry" (Luke 12:18-19).

Bigger barns. Eat, drink and be merry. Can you hear it? The emphasis was all on himself—comfort, security, ease. For him, money was only a vehicle for getting what he wanted for himself. His biggest concern was how he could spend the rest of his life lying around on a hammock.

Jesus didn't mince words. He called the man a fool. The manager had stored up things for himself but was not rich toward God. Where was the man's compassion? Where was his sense of purpose? Where was the sharing of his wealth with others? Where was the justice his money could have provided for others? Where did taking care of widows and orphans enter into the equation? (See James 1:27.)

The very night the manager articulated his selfish goals, his life was demanded of him. He kicked the bucket and died. A lot of good his money did him then.

Christ showed a different way of looking at money. In the same passage of Scripture, He tells all who follow Him not to worry about their lives, what they eat or drink or wear. Look at the birds of the air, Christ says—they have no storerooms, barns or bank accounts, yet God feeds them anyway. And how much more valuable are you than birds? (See Matt. 6:25-27.) Christ says that we are not to set our heart on what we eat or drink—just don't worry about it. People run after those things, but God knows you need stuff to live.

Here's one of the most famous verses in all of Scripture. It's repeated in Luke 12:31.

But seek first his kingdom and his righteousness, and these things will be given to you as well (Matt. 6:33).

In other words, let your pursuit of God be number one in your life. Everything falls into place when this happens. It's not that you seek God in order to get rich—that's not the emphasis here. Christ is saying let your priorities be on spiritual matters.

We know a man who has followed this principle his whole life. He has worked in a variety of churches, Christian camps and universities throughout his career. Any place he worked, he committed to seeking Christ first. In fact, he chose never to negotiate his salary. He never wanted to make money a factor in what the Lord led him to do. He and his wife raised two boys—everyone always seemed to have enough money for life's necessities. The kids both went to college. Yet when this man retired four years ago, the highest annual salary he had ever made was $30,000. (At the writing of this book, the average family wage is about $60,000.)

Here's the twist. When this man was beginning his career in the early 1960s, he and his wife bought a small beachfront shack for $12,500. They sold it 10 years later for $95,000 and bought another small beachfront house where they lived for the next 30 years. One month ago, they put their home on the market, intending to downsize in their retirement. The asking price? $2.2 million.

Did you catch that? Here's a guy who has never made more than thirty grand a year now selling his house for more than two million bucks. There's no way he could ever have afforded that type of house. That's God's upside-down economics—seek first the kingdom of God and everything else falls into place.

We want to be careful here, too, because this type of financial windfall doesn't happen with everybody who follows Christ. People twist Scripture to claim that when you follow

Christ wholeheartedly, you're guaranteed to become wealthy. But that's never specifically promised to us. Earthly wealth is not Christ's emphasis. Jesus always points people to align their hearts with what God considers valuable—treasures in heaven. Sometimes financial rewards come with that. Sometimes not. The point is to be wise about money—not to seek it as a goal, but to use it when we need it, and not worry about it along the way.

There are two other principles in Scripture that help us find the balance in the area of finances. The first is found in Psalm 50:10—God owns "the cattle on a thousand hills." The second is from Philippians 4:19—"God will meet all your needs according to his glorious riches in Christ Jesus."

In other words, we have nothing to worry about. God's got a lot of cows, and He's not afraid to share the wealth. One summer during college, I (Marcus) worked at a camp. I could have made way more money if I had worked construction again. But I was pretty sure the Lord wanted me at camp, even though I wasn't positive how I was going to pay for college that fall.

I started college without all my financial ducks in order. A few weeks after the beginning of classes, I "just happened" to read on a campus bulletin board that any student who worked at a summer camp was eligible for a one-time scholarship. Right away, I walked over to the financial aid center. They made some calls, and literally half an hour later I walked out with several thousand dollars in financial aid—more than I would have made if I had worked construction. If God leads you to a ministry, He'll provide the way to pay for it.

Faith and money can be a tricky combination. Sometimes God provides in unexplainable ways. But most often He works through natural courses. Even when we're seeking first the kingdom of God, Christ doesn't say that we should never think about money. Plenty of verses in Scripture instruct us in this area. Solomon's Proverbs are filled with directives.

Proverbs 1:19 tells us that being greedy for money robs you of your life. Proverbs 10:16 says that the earnings of the godly enhance their lives. In Proverbs 11:28, it says that if you trust in your money, you will go down. Proverbs 22:26-27 warns against being a cosigner on a loan; and Proverbs 22:7 notes that a person who borrows is always a slave to a person who lends. Solomon wrote in Ecclesiastes 5:10 that those who love money will never have enough—their wealth will be meaningless. And in Ecclesiastes 5:14, he writes that if money is put into risky investments, there will be nothing left in the end.

The truth is that money can't be ignored. Even though we're to seek God's kingdom and His righteousness first, that doesn't mean we're to be ignorant about money or how it works. Christ always calls us to live lives of wisdom. There's probably a case to be made for people who claim to live "too much" on faith, while ignoring the pragmatic tools that Christ gives us for operating in daily life. It's like the old illustration of a man stuck on a roof during a flood. The man prays that God will save him. Along comes a rescue worker with a raft who offers the stranded man a lift. "Nah, God will save me," says the man. So the raft passes him by. Along comes another rescue worker in a boat who offers to save the stranded man, who again turns it down, saying, "God will save me." Finally comes a helicopter with another offer to help. Again, the stranded man turns down the offer. "God will save me," he repeats. So the waters come up, the stranded man drowns and goes to heaven. "God, why didn't You save me?" asks the man.

"I did," God says. "I sent a raft, a boat and a helicopter. You turned me down."

This type of thinking happens in real life. We know a man who decided it was God's will for him and his family to live "on faith." He was skilled as a carpenter, but turned down jobs, believing that "God would provide." Money grew tight, and the family, which included five children, moved into a two-bedroom trailer house. They ate from handouts and soup kitchens. Two of the kids slept in the kitchen. Two kids shared a room, and the oldest daughter, about 14, slept on a mat in her parents' bedroom—which undoubtedly made things awkward for everybody.

We want to be careful in how we say this—because maybe there were other circumstances we didn't know about in that man's family—but it seemed that God would tell this man to accept the jobs that were coming his way and provide for his family, using the natural means of a job. Faith doesn't negate action, practical sense or wisdom. God expects you to live in the culture you're in. If you're living in the hills in remotest Haiti, it will probably work for you to live in a grass hut with no running water or electricity. But if you live in suburban North America, your city's building inspector will have some issues if you try to do the same. You need a job to make money so that you can get an apartment to live in.

Christ always calls us to be both faithful and wise. Yes—seek first God's kingdom, and everything else will fall into place. That's faith. Your money is all up to God.

At the same time, yes—learn how money works, and use it wisely. That's wisdom. Don't be ignorant about money or pretend it doesn't exist. Educate yourself on budgeting, investing, tithing, saving and credit issues.

God's call is always to use both faith *and* wisdom. Use both in balance.

GETTING PUNCHED
Gadgets, Credit Cards, Empty Pockets

Here's why it's hard to be a young man when it comes to money: It's because Pong doesn't cut it anymore.

Remember Pong? Along with Asteroids, Frogger and Space Invaders, it ruled the video game market for about a year.

Then disaster struck—as well as opportunity—when the shiny new Commodore 64 came out. Whoa, suddenly that old Atari just wasn't going to make the grade. The Commodore 64 embodied all the superlatives—the newest, coolest, brightest, whitest, most awesome video game system around. You had to have it.

Then along came Nintendo. And you had to have that too. Then Nintendo 64. Then that sucked because PlayStation came along. That got old when Xbox came out. Then it was Play-Station 2, then Xbox 360. Somewhere in that lineup was the Nintendo GameCube.

We're not video game historians, so maybe our lineup isn't quite precise, but the point is that you just can't win when it comes to technology. What you have today is already old. As soon as you buy something, you need what's next. Advertisers love us guys. Why? Because we're suckers for whatever new is around the corner.

There are at least three main punches that come fast at young men in the area of money:

- The first, as mentioned above, is having all those depreciating gadgets pushed at you. There's always a commercial somewhere telling you that you need to consume the newest car, electronic device or fast-food meal. It doesn't get any easier the older you get. About half my (Shaun's) garage is filled with junk we don't use anymore. There's the treadmill we used once. The computer desk that turned out to be garbage. What else? Just piles of junk we once thought were so important. All it does now is take up space.

- Second is credit offers pushed on you, even though you're hardly ever shown that you can use it wisely. I (Shaun) got my first credit card right away in college. I had no idea what to do with it other than buy a bunch of stuff I wanted and pay the lowest amount I could each month. Not a good recipe for success.

- Third is that you think you're too poor to manage your money wisely, so you don't learn the backbone of solid financial management: budgeting, saving, investing and tithing. You're too poor to think about money, right?

Wrong. The following are true situations from guys we've known through ministry. The names have been changed to maintain anonymity, but see if you can relate to any of the following situations.

- Right out of high school, Travis bought a brand-new Xterra, using a five-year car loan. To make the payments, he got a job at a grocery store and lived with his parents. Two years into the loan, Travis decided to go to college. He needed money. When he went to sell the vehicle, he found that the truck had depreciated steeply. In fact, he found that he actually owed more on the SUV than he could sell it for. He ended up working more hours at the grocery store and postponing college for two more years so that he could pay down his truck loan.

- On Colin's first day of college as a freshman, he was offered a credit card while standing in the orientation line. It seemed like a good idea at the time—credit card companies only loan money to people who can pay it back—right? When he got his first bill, all it said to do was pay the minimum payment, only $25. Using the card was so convenient—gas for his car, fast food late at night, shirts, textbooks, pizzas out with his dorm buddies. Colin never paid down his balance—it didn't seem to be required. After four years of college, Colin was more than $8,500 in credit card debt and had nothing to show for it. Plus he was paying a whopping 21 percent interest.

• At 22, Ike lived paycheck to paycheck. He had just landed his first job, and things were tight; but he opted for his own apartment and plenty of continual payment items such as cable TV, high-speed Internet and subscription radio. All was smooth until his transmission dropped out on the way to work one morning. Suddenly, his paycheck didn't stretch that far. How was he going to pay the $2,500 to get his car fixed?

• Rob had no idea what he wanted to do when he went to college. He majored in English, then switched to psychology, and finally graduated with a sociology degree. He liked the course work, but it wasn't exactly a highly marketable degree. Problem was, he had taken out wads of student loans along the way. He graduated with $45,000 in student loans and no hope for an immediate job. Even when he did land a job, it was only for 50 cents an hour over minimum wage. In his specific career field, it was going to take him a lifetime to pay back his student loans.

• Tyler loved stuff. Whatever it was, he bought it. His parents had plenty of money, so it seemed only natural that he live up to their level of consumption, particularly when he lived at home. Pretty much, he bought whatever he wanted, whenever he wanted it. When he moved out on his own, he was sorely shocked to discover how hard it was to make it without his parent's financial backing. The money he made as a young man could never begin to fund the type of lifestyle he was used to. But it didn't make sense to him. His parents had all this stuff, why should he go without? He ended up moving back in with his folks.

- As a young man, Ryan thought he didn't need health insurance. His job didn't provide any, and he was never sick, so why bother spending the chunk of money each month on something he'd never need. Then Ryan got into a car accident—nothing huge, but he broke his collarbone, knocked out his front teeth and split his palette. Without health insurance, his medical bills spiraled past $25,000. How was he ever going to pay those off?

The punches come at you fast. When it comes to money, faithfulness and wisdom go hand in hand. So how are you supposed to make it as a young man when it comes to the area of finances? How do you develop the code of financial responsibility?

TRUE TOUGHNESS
Your Coffee or a New Car?

How do you develop a wise, skillful approach to finances? We're going to take this subject by subject. Finances are one of those areas you will keep learning about little by little as the years go on. That's certainly the way it is with us.

Let's start with an easy one: spending.

Spending

When people tell you about money, they usually ignore this one. It's taken as a given that you've got to spend money. And usually the only directive here is to stop spending. Or don't spend as much as you take in.

But really, have you ever thought that spending money can be a good thing? At its core, money is a tool. Money in and of itself is just a blip on a computer screen, or it's a wad of green paper or a round circular hunk of metal. Money only becomes worthwhile when it can be exchanged for something.

So what's of value to you? Education? Transportation? Necessities such as food and clothing? Helping other people? It's okay to make and spend money. Maybe this sounds obvious, but we think it isn't. The love of money is wrong, but money in and of itself isn't wrong. Money is just a tool. No more, no less.

We need to repeat this again. Money is a tool, and it's okay to spend it to live. But the key with spending—and we can't say this loudly enough—is to spend less than you earn. It's so simple that it sounds stupid to say it. But you'd be surprised how few people do it.

Budgeting

Budgeting simply means that you allocate money for certain things. You decide how to spend the money you have, rather than let stuff or impulses decide for you. You've probably heard that it's important to budget, but do you actually do it? Budgeting is the key that almost everything else in this code hinges on. It doesn't matter what type of budget you develop. What's important is that you know what's coming in and where it's going.

Here's one way, called the envelope method. It's an easy, practical and hands-on approach to budgeting.

1. Estimate how much money you'll need for each group of expenses each month. Make up whatever categories are true to your life. It might be: gasoline, car repairs, food, entertainment, clothes, insurance, rent, etc. You might need to track your expenses for a month or two and tweak the amounts accordingly.

2. Get a box of envelopes and write the name of each of your spending categories on an envelope—each category on a separate envelope.

3. Whenever you get your paycheck, cash it and put in each envelope the amount of cash you've previously decided goes into that envelope. When you need money for an item, just pull out the envelope from that category and spend away. If there's no money in that envelope, then don't spend.

The only challenge with the envelope system is that cash isn't used much anymore. Guys use debit cards, credit cards or checkbooks. But don't let this deter you. If an actual envelope system doesn't work for you, create a virtual one, with a running balance for each category. There are also a variety of software programs that can do this for you.

The deal with a budget is to avoid excuses. Find one that works for you. Even if you're not making much money.

Savings

Saving is different from investing. Savings are used for several things: (1) accumulating funds so that you don't have to buy things on credit; (2) emergencies, such as your car overheating and your engine exploding; (3) a rainy-day fund for things you haven't quite figured out yet what they're going to be, but you just know you're going to need to buy them in the future, like Christmas gifts each December or a plane ticket home each spring.

What's the key with savings? It comes back to your budget. Decide your goals, then allocate a certain amount per month toward those goals.

And don't stick the money under your mattress, either. At the very least, stick the money in a savings account in the bank where it will earn interest.

Better yet is something called a Money Market account. This is like a savings account except the holder of your money invests your money in short-term securities, which typically gives you a higher interest rate. Your bank will offer Money Market accounts, as will most major investment firms such as Charles Schwab, T. Rowe Price, Fidelity or Edward Jones.

Investing

Most guys blow off investing. It's something you only do when you're older, right?

Wrong. Here's a simple truth. The earlier you start, the better off you'll be.

Investing simply means that you put aside money and expect to see a profit over time. There is no one way of investing. You can buy a house with the idea that it will go up in value, or a stack of rare coins or a group of mutual funds. The point is that you educate yourself about various types of investing, and then do it.

Typically, two great long-term investments are these: home ownership and mutual fund investments.

1. Buying a House

Conventional wisdom holds that there will always be more people in the world, but there's only a limited amount of space— so housing markets will almost always rise.

But it's not easy to sell a home once you've got it, so buying a house is usually a wise investment only if you're going to stay in one place for at least five years, which is typically why most guys don't buy houses—you're just not around any one place that long. So you've got to think about buying a house as something you'll do somewhere in your late 20s or early 30s. It's probably a decision that's a few years away right now, but there are still steps you can take today toward it.

Advertisers would have you believe that guys need to buy cool cars and live wherever, but really it's the other way around. Your car is a depreciating asset—it loses money. A house is an appreciating asset—it will (almost always) make you money. So it makes sense to limit the amount of money you spend on a car so that you can save for a house.

One of the wisest things you can do in the area of housing expenses is to live with housemates as long as you can. If a one-bedroom apartment rents for $900, a two-bedroom is usually not much more than that. If you live by yourself, you pay for it all on your own. If you've got a roommate, your housing bill is cut in half. Find an additional roommate, and suddenly your housing expenses are cut in thirds. I (Marcus) got married at age 29. I lived with housemates until seven months before I got married. It wasn't always easy, but it was definitely cheaper that way. And sometimes it could be a blast. One year, a bunch of us rented a big old house across the street from a lake. Five to eight people lived there, depending on the month. We'd have food fights that raged for days. One time we hung a barbecue from the second story window because we all wanted to eat upstairs. It's a wonder we didn't burn the joint down.

2. Mutual Funds and Stocks

Stocks are like owning pieces of businesses. When the business makes money, so do you. Mutual funds are groups of stocks.

You can buy investments such as these directly through broker-ages or through investment firms such as Edward Jones, which is typically easier and safer if you don't know much about how it all works. In America, there are also a variety of savings plan systems such as IRAs (Investment Retirement Account) that let you save money long-term while paying reduced or no taxes.

It's easy to think of investing long-term as something you only do when you get older. But the younger you start investing, the more you have later on. This is through the miracle of com-pound interest. You don't need to know a lot of math, just know stuff like this: If you contribute $100 per month to a retirement account, starting at age 25, you'd have about $379,000 by age 60. If you wait 10 years and start saving at age 35, still putting $100 in, you'll have only $132,000 when you're 60.[1]

Let's raise the stakes a bit. If you contribute $4,000 a year toward retirement beginning at age 23, you'll have about $1 million in 40 years, assuming an 8 percent growth rate. But wait just 5 years to begin, at age 28, even though you contribute the same amount, your nest egg in 40 years shrinks by 33 per-cent, to about $690,000. It's crucial to start young. A good rule of thumb is to invest at least 10 percent of your earnings to-ward retirement.

When I (Marcus) was a youth pastor, one of my high school students worked a summer job and opened a retirement ac-count at the end of the summer with about $2,000. His dad showed him how to do it. The kid was only 16, and some of his buddies gave him a hard time for it, saying he was thinking like an old fuddy-duddy. But that kid was totally wise. By the time he's 65, that small investment will be huge.

Think you don't have enough money to invest?

One of the great places to look for "extra" money is in those small, regular purchases. They can really add up. Let's just say you're in the habit of getting a latte every morning that costs

$4. It's just a cup of coffee, right? But in a week you've spent $28. In a month you've spent $120; and in a year you've spent a whopping $1,460 . . . on *coffee*. You just drank away the equivalent of a wide-screen TV.

Here's where those regular expenditures really add up. If you took that same $4 a day spent on coffee and invested that in a good mutual fund that earns 8 percent annually (most do), in 10 years you'd have about $20,000.[2] Basically, enough for a new car. So it's coffee or a new car—you decide.

Credit

Today, you pretty much need credit. It's almost impossible to buy a house without it. And it's almost impossible to buy a car without it.

To get credit, you need to develop it, and this is where a lot of people get into trouble, because the easiest way of developing credit is to get a credit card (or at the very least a gas card) or a small consumer loan from a bank. People get into trouble because they don't pay their loans back, or they pay them back late or only pay their minimum balance on credit cards. The rule is this: If you get a loan, absolutely pay it back in the time you agreed to. And if you get a credit card, absolutely always pay your monthly balance in full. Never just pay the minimum balance. You'll get hosed in sky-high interest payments.

Remember how in elementary school there was all this fear associated with "your permanent record"—whatever that was. Like, if you blew an exam or punched another kid in the nose or missed too many days of school, it would be on *your permanent record.*

Well, a permanent record actually does exist, in a manner of speaking. It's called your credit score. It lasts for about seven years. And you're constantly generating one even though you might not realize it.

Your three-numbered credit score is developed and shaped every time you open a bank account, apply for a credit card or car loan, pay bills or don't pay bills, change addresses, and lots more. It's the history of how you use money. In America, your score is primarily based on information given to and received from three major credit bureaus called Experian, Transunion and Equifax. Lenders, employers and landlords typically supply the information to the bureaus. By law, you're entitled to check your credit score once a year for free. You can check it as often as you want, but it usually costs you $15 to $20 each time.

Why is your credit score important? Because potential lenders, landlords, insurance companies, employers and state agencies can view your score and decide how trustworthy you are. Your score can determine whether you get a loan, a job or how much you'll pay for a particular item. You want a good credit score.

For instance, if you've got a great credit score, like 720-850, you might pay 6.6 percent interest for a car loan. But if have a junky credit score, like 500-589, you might pay a whopping 18 percent interest. Same car, you'll just pay way more for it.[3]

How do you get a great credit score? A variety of methods exist for fine-tuning your credit score, and if you Google around you'll find them. Just type in "increase credit score." The simplest one boils down to this: Pay all of your bills on time. Always.

Bottom line, developing credit is something you need to do as you get older. Credit isn't the enemy. You've just got to use it wisely.

Tithing
Last, but certainly not least, is tithing. The word "tithe" means "a tenth." In the Old Testament, that amount was required. In this age, it's a ballpark figure. Tithing is when you set aside some of your resources on a regular basis to give specifically to

God. There are no hard-and-fast rules on tithing—it's all about your heart's attitude. You can tithe to a church, to a parachurch organization like a camp or missions organization, to an international relief agency such as Compassion International or World Vision, or directly to a person in need. Simply handing a homeless person a $5 bill might be a tithe if you're giving the money in Jesus' name.

A bunch of debates exist right now over how much you should tithe, what happens when you do, and even over whether or not you should tithe in the first place. Save yourself a headache and stay out of the debates. Here are some of the principles set out in Scripture.

Deuteronomy 8:10-20 lays the foundation for giving to God. It's all about remembering what the Lord has given you. It's about wanting to be part of His plan and purposes. It's about using your money wisely, for things that matter.

Proverbs 3:9-10 says to honor the Lord first. Some people take this literally and make sure that the first check they write every month is to God. With others, it's more a heart attitude.

Malachi 3:10 talks about giving to God wholeheartedly, not holding back, and that there really is a blessing when you give to God. Some people use this verse as a guarantee that God will bless them financially when they give to Him, but really it's more a general principle, not an investment strategy. We can never outgive God.

Matthew 6:2-4 is on the subject of giving silently to God—not making a big deal about it, not calling attention to yourself.

Second Corinthians 9:7 says that the Lord loves a cheerful giver. The word "cheerful" actually means "hilarious" in the original language—God loves it when you give to Him with a big grin on your face.

Will you give some of your income to God? No one will force you to do this, but really, it's in your best interest to do so. At a very basic level, the spiritual institutions that you're part of can't survive unless people give money to them. If you want a good college group, if you want your pastor to be able to feed his family, then someone's got to give. But it's more than that. When you tithe, you recognize the big principle of the code of financial responsibility: that all you have is His. Tithing is a good thing.

DEVELOPING YOUR CODE
On the Line

The code of financial responsibility is one that's often developed over time. This may be a chapter you want to read and think about for a month or two, even a year or two, then go back and reread. Often, you implement suggestions for financial responsibility bit by bit. That's okay. Think of this book as a basic blueprint. You'll want to add to it as time goes on.

In the meantime, let's do some work right now on this code. Work through these questions by yourself, with a small group of trusted guys, or one on one with a mentor.

1. At the start of this chapter, Shaun said, "Only when you release what you have back to Him does life makes sense." What might that look like in the area of your finances?

2. What's the hardest thing about money for you?

3. Wisdom and faithfulness go hand in hand. What does that mean?

4. What is one step you can take this week toward greater financial responsibility?

Notes
1. "Should You Save for Retirement at a Young Age?" *Money Crashers,* September 4, 2007. http://www.moneycrashers.com/should-you-save-for-retirement-at-a-young-age/ (accessed October 2007).
2. "Stop Buying Expensive Coffee and Save Calculator," *Hugh's Mortgage and Financial Calculators.* http://www.hughchou.org/calc/coffee.cgi (accessed October 2007).
3. Lee Ann Obringer, "How Credit Scores Work," *How Stuff Works.* http://money.how stuffworks.com/credit-score2.htm (accessed October 2007).

ONE THING TO THINK ABOUT:

WHEN IT COMES TO MONEY, BE BOTH FAITHFUL AND WISE.

DEVELOP YOUR CODE FROM HERE.

LONG-HAUL FAITH
THE CODE OF BEST PRACTICES

Two mistakes I've (Marcus) made in my life are these: thinking that I'd be a high school rugby god forever, and believing that too much frozen pizza would never do me wrong.

To explain . . .

In high school, staying in shape never seemed a problem for me. I ran track, played volleyball, basketball and rugby, and walked everywhere I went. I was always moving. But in college, sports slowed down while all the pressures of life escalated: exams, girlfriends, figuring out what I wanted to do for the rest of my years—it all added up. By the time my junior year rolled around, I found myself puking most mornings. This was a real drag, to say the least. So I went to the doctor.

"Do much regular exercise?" he asked.

"Sure," I said. "I ride a bike and snow ski."

"How often?"

"Well, I ride about once a week and ski maybe three or four times a season."

"There's your problem," the doctor said. "You're out of shape."

I was only 20. Turns out that I had developed an inflammation of the duodenum, the small tube off your stomach where a lot of digestion takes place. Basically, I had the beginnings of an ulcer. Too much stress, the doctor concluded, and not enough regular—and by regular he meant *daily*—exercise in my life to burn off all that stress. I wasn't a high school rugby god anymore.

A couple of years later, I worked as a youth pastor. To be a good youth pastor, I figured I needed to hang out with high school kids a lot. So I went to high school games, spent time at high schools and congregated wherever high school students did—mostly at Dairy Queen. I ate gobs of banana splits, Oreo Blizzards and Dilly Bars. On a rare evening when I had dinner at home, I'd pop in a frozen pizza or pick up some burgers at the drive-thru. I was doing a lot of running at the time, so I wasn't packing on the pounds from my junky diet, but I always had this crazy runny nose thing—just sort of a slow-drip beak faucet. It wasn't quite a cold, but I never really felt healthy either. So I went to the doctor again.

"Exercising every day?" he asked.

"Yep," I said. "I walk. I run. I'm a regular moving machine."

"How about those fruits and vegetables?" he asked. "Eat much of that kind of thing?

"Um," I said, "do French fries count?"

The frozen pizzas had done me wrong. Turns out that I had developed food allergies from eating the same junk over and over. My body's immune system was all but shot. I was only in my mid 20s and already starting to show signs of wearing down. The doctor put me on a restricted diet where I had to learn how to cook something other than microwave dinners. Gradually, I healed up.

Here's what this chapter is about—living like there's a tomorrow. Why? Because ready or not, tomorrow comes; and you want to be strong your whole life. So, what are the sustainable habits that lead to lifelong leadership and maturity? How can you prevent burning out, clogging up or falling off track?

Christians can be notorious for ignoring this. We're typically encouraged to be hard chargers for God, and we mistakenly think the road to godliness lies in ignoring fitness, health and true leisure activity. We don't think it's spiritual enough. How many fat, flabby pastors do you know? How many workaholic spiritual leaders are out there? How many dudes are following Christ with all they've got but are inadvertently leading hopelessly imbalanced lives filled with 16-hour workdays and fueled with bellyfuls of Taco Bell and Red Bull?

If you want to have true fervor for the life God invites you to lead, you can't ignore tomorrow. You've got to develop your code of best practices now. Consider these the disciplines that let you move past running sprints to all-out marathons. Primarily, these disciplines relate to three sides of your life: physical, mental (which often includes emotional) and spiritual.

The big question here is how can you succeed over the long haul. The answer might involve turning down the king's food and eating some pulse.

CHISELED TRAINING
Eating Pulse

In many ways, the pattern of Jesus' life is the opposite of what the lives of many of today's spiritual leaders look like. Jesus was never impressed by a clock. He didn't carry a pocket calendar. He often chose to ignore huge crowds of people and go off by Himself to be alone (see Mark 6:32). He sometimes slept when others were working (see Mark 4:38). It took Him 30 years to prepare for a 3-year ministry (see Luke 3:23). He had developed His code of best practices and found the balance between intensity and rest.

Simply put, Jesus was never a workaholic. But Jesus wasn't a slacker either. He knew what it was like to work hard, and His life could be characterized by extreme intensity. He wasn't afraid to jump into a battle (see Matt. 23). He often ministered to huge numbers of people (see Mark 8). Sometimes He spent all night in prayer (see Luke 6:12-16). Jesus' life was a pattern for healthy living. He had developed a strategy for life, and that meant working hard but not being wound up tighter than a $3 watch.

That's what we're talking about here—the code of "best practices." What exactly is that term all about? A friend of ours, we'll call him Randy the Brainy Dude, spent quite a few years as a computational physicist. He switched careers and works full-time as a novelist now, but over the years he's done quite a bit of scientific software consulting.

According to Randy the Brainy Dude, people in the software industry use the phrase "best practices" a lot. It's part of the jargon in software analysis, design and implementation. A "best practice" is a technique known to produce superior results to solve a particular problem. Sometimes there is more than one best practice for a given type of problem, and in that case, you get to choose among them. But you definitely want to stay away from "worst practices," says Randy the Brainy Dude. So take his word for it, not ours.

When talking about maturity, another term for best practices is "self-discipline." It's not the same thing as self-control, like we talked about in chapter 2, which is about living by intentionality as opposed to living by impulse. Rather, self-discipline is about living with an eye to the future. It's choosing the best practices that allow you to have sustainable ministry and leadership. Jesus developed this code. He knew what it meant to live healthily.

Another good example of some guys who developed their code for best practices is found in the book of Daniel. As the story goes, a young Hebrew named Daniel and his buddies Hananiah, Mishael and Azariah are living in the country of Judah when it happens to get overrun by King Nebuchadnezzar and the armies of Babylon.

Nebuchadnezzar kicks the stew out of Judah, and he plunders all the spoils of victory—all their gold, silver, treasures, animals and weapons. He also steals one of the most valuable resources of any country—its young people. By taking this action, Nebuchadnezzar ensures that a defeated country grows up weak, and that conversely, his country grows up strong. He steals the future.

Put this into perspective. Imagine it's World War II, and Adolph Hitler and Nazi Germany win the war. They sweep into America and round up all the high-achieving teenagers, then cart them back to the Fatherland and begin to indoctrinate them in the ways of Nazism. That way, all the young Americans grow up thinking the thoughts of Adolph Hitler. Nazism rises in power while democracy falls. This is what happened to Daniel and his three friends. Nebuchadnezzar corralled all the "young men without any physical defect, handsome, showing aptitude for every kind of learning, well informed, quick to understand, and qualified to serve in the king's palace" (Dan. 1:4). The youths were put on a three-year schedule to "learn the language and literature of the Babylonians," and then they entered the service of the king.

As part of the indoctrination, Daniel and his friends were supposed to eat all the rich food of Babylon. We're not exactly sure what kind of food it was, but it's a safe bet that the food was contrary to the strict dietary laws of the Hebrews. So Daniel made a decision "not to defile himself with the royal food and wine" (Dan. 1:8). Tactfully, Daniel asked permission to eat the healthy food he was used to. Some translations call this food "vegetables," but really the original word is "pulse." Daniel asked to eat shovelfuls of "pulse." Again, we're not sure what this was, but think of a strong heartbeat (i.e., "pulse") as an indication of health.

At first, the chief official assigned to guard Daniel and his friends balked when he considered their request. If Daniel and his buddies started to look sick, it would mean lights out for the chief official. But Daniel proposed a 10-day food test. At the end of the test, they'd get a check-up. If Daniel and his friends were healthier from eating pulse, so be it. But if they looked less healthy, then Daniel and his buddies would eat the king's Big Macs as originally planned.

The chief official agreed to the test. Daniel and his buddies ate pulse for 10 days and all looked like young Schwarzeneggers. The Bible records that "At the end of the ten days they looked healthier and better nourished than any of the young men who ate the royal food" (Dan. 1:15). The healthy choices paid off, and Daniel and his friends went on to have significant careers in the king's service, even though they were in Babylon. They were able to keep their integrity intact and go on to do amazing things for God.

What's the point? Your long-term health—physical, spiritual and mental—is one key ingredient of maturity. Simply, what you eat affects your performance. If you fill up on root beer and Coco Puffs, you're bound to be frosty and sugar-coated. If you fill up on healthy stuff, things such as leadership and maturity fall more easily into place.

The type of food you eat is only one part of developing your code of best practices. Paul says in 1 Corinthians 9:21-24 to run a race like you want to win it. Run with purpose in every step. What does that look like for your life when you consider tomorrow, not just today? How can you have the endurance you need for all parts of your life?

GETTING PUNCHED
Sloth and Burnout: Both Are Easy

Here's what's tough about being a guy.

In the area of leisure, guys often can be either one extreme or another. Guys are either super hard-chargers and don't know how to pace themselves in work, sports, school or ministry. Or else they're couch-sitting potatoes, happiest with a Coke, a smile and 12 hours of video games.

Neither is a best practice. When I (Marcus) went to seminary, I saw this principle embodied. All of us crammed our heads chock full of knowledge. There wasn't a guy I knew who wasn't a hard-charger when it came to his brain. But so many dudes graduated from seminary with their heads full of good stuff while their bodies were wrecked and flabby. Having a heart attack at age 25 because your arteries are full of cheese pizzas is not the key to lasting effectiveness.

It's also easy to fall into extremes in your spiritual life. Maybe you go to a camp or spiritual retreat and get all pumped up for God. You vow to read straight through Leviticus and pray on your knees for three hours every morning at 4 A.M. But when Monday after the retreat comes, the snooze button is just too inviting. Quickly you fall back into a habit of spiritual nonchalance. Your Bible sits unopened. Your prayers are infrequent. Your heart is distant from God.

Physical health is another area where the punches come fast. Eating junk food now and then is not wrong, but when you're young, it's everywhere: every party, every dorm room, every youth-group event, every after-school snack, every late-night Taco Bell run. It's so easy to fall into the habit of always eating fast food. And health goes beyond what you eat. Once you stop taking PE classes in school, it becomes a lot harder to be self-disciplined in that area. Maybe your mother signed you up every fall for soccer, but she doesn't do that anymore. Maybe your buddies and you played pick-up basketball every afternoon, but now your buddies are working part-time jobs, studying or trying to land a killer internship. Physical fitness is your responsibility now. How do you develop the code of best practices in your life?

I (Shaun) admit I am still learning this code in my life. I want to have intensity now, and not just as a young man, but for my whole life. In my job, it's so easy to burn the candle at both ends. There's always something that needs to be done. I'll go through stretches of days, weeks, even months when I'm not consciously listening to my body or my mind. The lack of balance shows up. When life is out of whack, I'm quick to get angry, impatient with people or mad at my staff. If I stop long enough, I can sense in my own heart there's something wrong. There's a direct correlation in my life between my attitude and how healthy I am. When I'm not healthy, my attitude goes out the window.

Just two weeks ago, I was the speaker at a retreat for a Christian school at Big Bear, in the mountains of Southern California. I spoke 4 times in 48 hours, which is pretty intense. But one of the cool things about the weekend for me was that I was able to get alone several times and just spend time with God. The second day of the retreat, I found an empty spot outdoors, built a fire and just sat and read my Bible. That's refreshment. I had the energy and perspective from time with God to finish the retreat well. I know that I need to build consistent times like this into my life. Often they happen, but it's easy to get sidetracked too.

For instance, in the area of physical fitness, I've always been athletic. I'm 6'2," built pretty solid and have always played sports. But once you're married, and particularly once you have kids, it's way tougher to find the time to stay fit. That's when all your muscles turn to mush. Years ago, when I was a youth pastor in Indiana, a friend challenged me in this area. He had been a starting Center at Ball State University, then he played pro ball for the Kansas City Chiefs. He had a weight room at his house, and we started to work out a couple of times each week. I found that I had really missed regular exercise. When I moved to Savannah, a guy at our church was a former Mr. Georgia.

He was still huge and owned a vitamin and supplement store. He put me on a workout plan and got me into vitamins and supplements. From there I moved to Southern California, where I still work out every morning. I love it. It's become fun. When I'm physically fit, I can fight off colds easier. I don't feel as sluggish. I have more energy. If I don't work out, I feel like a wet dishrag.

The key to this code is always keeping an eye on what's ahead. How can you be effective both now and for tomorrow? What practices and disciplines will you develop to ensure that you're going to make it for the long haul?

TRUE TOUGHNESS
The Sustainability Code

Let's break this down to a few specific components. First, in the area of physical fitness, what sort of regular exercise will you undertake to ensure long-term health?

I (Marcus) admit that I'm no Greek Adonis. But I stay fit. Like Shaun said, when I don't stay healthy, I can feel it. So I run two to three times a week, do pull-ups at a nearby park and walk every day after lunch for about 20 minutes. I still eat my share of ice cream, but I watch my intake of salt, fat and fried foods. I try to eat vegetables and fruit several times a day. Fitness is neither rocket science nor extreme with me; it's just part of the long-term pattern of my life.

Body
How about you? A good long-term exercise program should involve several components. The basics are these:

1. **Strength training.** You don't have to aim to get huge, but you do need to exercise your muscles on a regular

basis. Maybe this involves lifting weights or doing push-ups. Strength training is not the same as bodybuilding. Bodybuilding is a specific sport whose aim is to get ripped. Strength training is simply about exercising your muscles and increasing or maintaining your strength.

2. **Cardio.** This is where you exercise your heart and lungs on a regular basis. Maybe this is running, walking quickly, working out on a rowing machine, or riding a bike. You've got to get your heart rate up and keep it up there for a while to do any good.

3. **Eating right.** Entire books are devoted to this subject, but basically for a guy it comes down to this: Watch your intake of fast food and eat a balanced diet that includes plenty of fruits and vegetables. Stop drinking Mountain Dew and heavily sugared, caffeinated drinks all the time and switch to water, milk or juice.

4. **Flexibility.** This is often one of the hardest things for guys, because there's no immediate gain. A friend of ours is taking a flexibility class right now that his girlfriend is teaching. He was skeptical at first, but now he really likes the class. His comment: "I've never known I could move like that before." The goal is to stay limber.

5. **Having fun.** Staying fit doesn't have to be a drag. One of the things that help in this area is to have a goal in mind. You may not enjoy running, but maybe you love skiing. So you run throughout the off-season so that your quads are in shape when the snow falls.

Mind

What are the patterns that will ensure long-term success when it comes to your mind? A few suggestions:

1. **Sabbaths**. The idea of a Sabbath is simply to have regular breaks. Do something at least once a week that refreshes you. For instance, we know some guys who have made a point never to do homework on a Sunday. They push to get all their stuff done the other six days of the week. This is great. An old adage says a man can't do seven days' work in seven days, but he can do seven days' work in six days.

2. **Hobbies.** The older you get, the harder it can be to have hobbies. The other activities in your life start crowding in. But a good hobby can re-energize your mind. Sounds weird, but we know a pastor who carves tops—you know, those wood toys that kids spin around. He's got this woodworking lathe in a shop behind his house. Whenever the pressures of his job get to be too much, he goes out to his shop and carves some tops. He gives 'em to kids in the church and community. Why not?

3. **Reading**. Too many guys don't like to read, but this is a tragedy. The best ideas in the world are found in books. If ever you find yourself at a loss creatively, try opening a book. Maybe this sounds like the sort of advice your elementary school librarian would give you, but we're trying to be serious here: Real men read.

4. **Silence**. Some guys live with everything on loud. It doesn't matter if it's the car radio, the TV or the

normal conversations of everyday life. But part of a healthy life means allowing yourself the space for contemplation. What would your life look like if every once in a while you purposely turned everything off and gave your mind a rest?

Soul

You've probably heard the basics before. To maintain a growing relationship with God, you need to regularly read the Bible and pray. It's not about going through the motions; it's about constantly having a heart devoted to God.

Here are some things that I (Shaun) do in developing this code for myself and my staff. Every month I give my staff a day off for a spiritual retreat. There are no hard-and-fast rules for the day; it's simply a day to go out and feed your soul. That might mean sleeping in. It might mean not answering phones. It might mean going to a park and hanging out for a while, just you and God. Really, almost every activity can be done for the Lord. I've had staff members go see a movie on their spiritual retreat day, and I'm okay with that, as long as it had a purpose. What gets your mind relaxed and thinking thoughts of God? That's the start of a spiritual retreat day.

Personally, I've gotten into the habit of not saying "amen" whenever I pray. Prayer is hard with my ADD brain. I'm not the type of guy who prays for 10 hours straight. I just can't concentrate that long. But length of time shouldn't be the emphasis of prayer either. First thing when I wake up each morning, I start the day by praying to God. I'm still lying in bed at this point. I want to begin each day thinking about God. And then I don't say amen. The point is that prayer never stops throughout the day. If I'm merging into traffic, or waiting in line at a store, or answering the phone or whatever, I'm still in conversation with God. A lot of it is not out loud. It's my spirit communing with

God. At the end of the day, I'll consciously pray again, just to reflect back through the day's events with God. It's a heart attitude of always being in prayer with God.

Surely there's more to the area of maintaining your spiritual health over the long haul, but those are just a few thoughts to get your mind running.

DEVELOPING YOUR CODE
The Code of Tomorrow

How will you develop the code of best practices in your life? When you are out of shape as a leader—whether it's mental, physical or spiritual shape—you lose all fervor. You lose energy and focus. You're not at the top of your game. But when you're in shape, you feel confident for every challenge. You've got what it takes to make it through each punch that comes your way.

Again, this may be a chapter you want to read and think about for a month or two, even a year or two, then go back and reread. Often, you implement suggestions for your code of best practices bit by bit. That's okay. You don't have to do everything at once. Think of this book as a basic blueprint. You'll want to add to it as time goes on.

In the meantime, let's do some work right now on this code. Work through these questions by yourself, with a small group of trusted guys, or one on one with a mentor.

1. Why is it necessary to think not only about today but about the long-term as well?

2. What "best practice" do you currently succeed at most? In which area do you struggle most?

3. What is something you can do this week to help develop one best practice in your life?

ONE THING TO THINK ABOUT:

YOU WANT TO BE EFFECTIVE FOR THE LONG HAUL.

DEVELOP YOUR CODE FROM HERE.

BROTHERS

THE CODE OF MENTORING

What does it take to pass something along to someone younger than you?

At first glance, Earl Crawley, 69, better known as "Mr. Earl," makes an unlikely mentor, particularly in the area of finances. He earns only about $20,000 a year as a parking lot attendant—considered chicken feed in this day and age. But strangely enough, he's started an investment club at his church. He regularly coaches young men how to invest in stocks, bonds and mutual funds. Why would anyone listen to Mr. Earl?

A recent news article carried the story: When Mr. Earl was a young man, he took his share of punches. In school, he had dyslexia and was considered a slow learner. He was told he wouldn't amount to much in life. After graduating, he got a bottom-rung job at a bank. One of the senior bankers took him aside and leveled with him. "You don't have the education to go very far in this industry," said the senior banker, "but you've got what it takes to learn how to invest."

Mr. Earl took the advice to heart. "My true gift from God is my ability to listen," he says, "and that's how I was able to ask questions and use tips from the brokers, financial planners, and bank customers I saw every day."

As a young man, Earl learned how to budget. He saved what he could from taking odd jobs, such as lawn cutting and window washing, that he did in addition to his day job. As soon as he could, Mr. Earl began to buy stocks—always in tiny increments. For instance, he saved enough money to buy just one share of IBM stock when it was first issued.

The result?

Today, Earl's stock portfolio is worth more than $500,000. Not bad for someone whose annual income has always been under the poverty line. His message: "People can do whatever they set their minds to do." That's why he started the investment club at his church—to pass along what he's learned, and to encourage people younger than him.[1]

Have you ever thought you've got what it takes to be a mentor—even as a young man? Maybe you've never imagined yourself in this role. What do you know about anything? Maybe you've always thought you had to reach a certain age and stage before you could be considered for that role.

But really, every man is called to be a model to lead the next generation with honor, wisdom and compassion. As a man—even as a young man—you want to have mentors, and you want to be one yourself. This is something you can do your whole life: see the next generation with an eye to guidance.

CHISELED TRAINING
Thank You, Sir, May I Have Another?

Often, there's a mentality shift required when we begin to view the people around us within a mentorship grid. As young men, we're typically expected to scoff at younger guys, almost to bully them. We're supposed to be senior guys in a fraternity who take swats at the new pledges. Or we're like the seasoned beat cops blaming mistakes on the rookies. There's a false tough-guy mentality in play here—that because we've had to learn the ropes the hard way, by figuring out life for ourselves; there's no way we're going to give a younger guy a break.

The summer I (Marcus) worked construction, it was often this way. The older guys on the crew knew how it was done. We didn't. I often felt like I was a 17-year-old snot-nosed punk. One day the other grunt and I were called to haul away a bunch of old wall insulation. We spent all afternoon hefting the itchy junk around. Because it was summer, we were wearing short-sleeved shirts. At the end of our shift, our arms were covered in red welts from the fiberglass exposure. "Oh yeah," said the fore-man, "I should have told you guys to wear long shirts. There's also a cream you can put on your arms to keep the insulation out. You can wear it tomorrow." The older guys who heard this all guffawed. That's the way it was on crew. The older guys let you learn the hard way.

Maybe there's wisdom to that. There's a sense in which you can learn life's lessons by encountering natural consequences. Maybe the construction workers had tried to give advice to younger guys before and the young guys didn't pay attention. Who knows? All I know is that I went to bed that night with hot washcloths on my arms, trying to sweat out the fiberglass par-ticles. Personally, I think mentoring goes beyond that. The key is not only that you help the guys in your charge figure things out, but you have the highest concern for their growth and development. Whether that's by directly offering advice or by letting them learn lessons by themselves, the heart attitude is always one of passing along wisdom.

The Bible shows several examples of this type of mentoring in action.

In Exodus 18, Moses is hard at work, sitting as judge for all the people of Israel while they're out in the desert. The people "stood around him from morning till evening" (Exod. 18:13). When Moses' father-in-law, Jethro, heard about it, he took his son-in-law to task. "Why do you alone sit as judge, while all these people stand around you all day?" he asked.

"Because I'm the only one qualified to do it," Moses answered.

"That's a crock of manure," Jethro replied, or words to that effect.

So Jethro helped Moses figure out a better system of deciding disputes. Jethro told Moses to select capable men and have them decide the routine cases, then save the very hardest for himself. That way Moses would be able to last the long haul. Moses did what his father-in-law suggested, and everything went swell. It was an early example of Moses choosing the code of best practices that we talked about in the last chapter. It's also an example of mentoring. In this case an older guy, Jethro, shows a younger guy, Moses, how to live wisely.

In turn, Moses mentored a younger guy named Joshua, even before Moses had it all figured out. A chapter earlier than the Jethro scene, in Exodus 17, Moses led the Israelites into battle against the Amalekites. Joshua spearheaded the actual battle charge, but Moses was never far away. He stayed within eyesight of Joshua, pointing him to the source of victory. In the end, Moses gave Joshua directions to secure the final win. A few chapters later, in Exodus 24, Moses took Joshua with him up the mountain to receive the Ten Commandments. While Moses spoke with God directly, Joshua wasn't far away. The mentoring continued.

At the end of Moses' life, he led the Israelites out of Egypt, but he passed on the baton to Joshua. By then, Joshua had developed the skills necessary to lead the Israelites into the Promised Land.

Another example of mentoring is found in the story of Elijah and Elisha. Elijah, the older prophet, first meets Elisha in 1 Kings 19:19 where he sees the younger dude out plowing with oxen in a field. Elijah "threw his cloak" around Elisha. A mantle was the official uniform of a prophet. By throwing it on a younger man's shoulders, Elijah was singling out Elisha to follow in his footsteps. The mentorship had begun.

For the next chunk of time, Elisha followed Elijah around, watching how the older guy did it. Elisha received lessons in practical theology and caring for others. He learned humility, loyalty, faithfulness and obedience. He learned the tools and workings of his craft. Elisha learned how to become a true blood-and-thunder prophet, able to keep his cool in the midst of a degenerate, vicious and cruel season of the kingdom of Israel.

That's how it is with mentors. When you mentor someone, you care about how he turns out. You've turned the corner from bullying someone, even from simply having a guffaw at his expense, to helping him learn life's ropes. You want him to succeed. When he succeeds, that's a reflection of your leadership in his life. That's your call as a man.

But mentoring someone is not always easy.

GETTING PUNCHED
The Mikeys in Your Life

One of the challenges with mentoring is that perhaps no one mentored you. Or if someone did, maybe it was in a manner that caused you to sift through the chaff to see the kernel of truth he planted in your life.

My (Shaun's) relationship with my dad is a bit like this. Growing up, I knew he was a man who followed God. But he was also the type of guy who came from the generation that believed the best thing you could do as a man was throw yourself into your work. Because my dad was a pastor, there was always something to do at the church, so he simply wasn't around very much. He has admitted this as a mistake in later years. I don't ever remember throwing a baseball around with him. He never helped my mother around the house. He was just too busy all the time with church stuff. At age 16, I vowed that when I got married I'd make more time for my family and help my wife out around the home more. Hopefully I'm keeping both those commitments today. It can be hard to mentor someone when you've struggled with being mentored yourself.

Another challenge with mentoring is being annoyed with people younger than you. Depending on the person, it can require a real mindset shift to look past someone's shortcomings and want to help him out.

For instance, when I (Marcus) was growing up, there was a kid in my church who fit this description. I'll call him Mikey. He was about five years younger than me and completely freakishly into science. His parents were brainy sorts who had never talked to him as anything less than an equal, so Mikey conversed with the false intellectual vocabulary of a Ph.D. candidate. For fun, he loved to show everyone his collection of spiders, bugs and snakes. He was one of those kids that everyone just sort of tolerates.

Years passed, and I was on leadership staff at a camp. Who should sign up to be a counselor-in-training that summer but Mikey the Snakehandler. He had grown his hair long by then and claimed to be the answer to all rock 'n' roll's success questions, because he had taught himself guitar. But Mikey was desperately still a misfit. He had no idea how to act around girls. He told goofy jokes. He was still one of those kids that everybody just sort of puts up with. Here was my decision: I could help show Mikey the ropes, or I could go with my gut and pretend I didn't know him.

I can't say that Mikey and I ever became close friends. Fortunately, I had the maturity to know that this kid needed some guidance. I pulled some strings and got him hooked up with a good counselor partner who I knew would look out for him. Whenever I saw Mikey around camp, I tried to include him in conversations and activities. Basically, I just tried to treat him normally. It wasn't a formal sort of mentorship where I sat down with him every week and went through a Bible study, but it was a mindset shift. I wasn't going to bully this kid or whack him with a hazing bat or have him move insulation without wearing long sleeves. I was going to help Mikey out in whatever way I could.

I (Shaun) have a similar story. Being a mentor is easiest when you and the younger guy automatically sort of "get" each other. You connect naturally. But if you don't, it can take real maturity to figure out how to reach out and help someone along.

A kid in our youth ministry in Indiana fit this description. He was super short and chubby. He wore glasses and always had his shirt tucked in. He didn't play sports, and he loved tinkering with electronic stuff. Within the currency of today's youth culture, this guy was dead broke. I was nice to him in a cordial sort of way, but that was about it.

One week he was in my cabin at camp. All the dudes were unpacking their suitcases, just hanging out, and another dude decides to rip one. Pretty soon my whole cabin is flatulating up a storm. Except this kid. He's just sitting on his bunk really quiet like, holding his nose.

Funny what can move you from the outside of a circle in. During a lull in the action, this quiet kid worked out a squeaker. He ripped it and sat there with this proud look on his face, and then he laughed a sort of nerdy giggle. All the rest of the guys were completely silent for a moment; I think we were all shocked. Then we roared with laughter. It was like all of us realized at once that this kid who loved floppy disks was normal after all. He could rip with the best of us. One joke broke the barrier. From that point on, our relationship was different. He got involved. He got connected. Guys accepted him as one of the group. He ended up building our whole youth website.

What sort of challenges will you need to overcome to make mentoring a regular part of your life?

TRUE TOUGHNESS
Mindset Shift

What we don't want to give you in this chapter is a step-by-step primer for developing a mentoring relationship with a younger dude. If you're involved with a ministry situation at your church or youth group, chances are they'll have some good practical advice for doing that.

What we do want to do is help instill the code of mentoring as one of the best practices of your life. Call this a mindset shift. No matter where you are or what you do, you look at the next generation of guys as people you can help. Instead of thinking life is all about your dreams and ambitions, you see that it's also about helping the next generation too. Mentoring is where you can echo the words of the psalmist:

> Since my youth, O God, you have taught me, and to this day I declare your marvelous deeds. Even when I am old and gray, do not forsake me, O God, till I declare your power to the next generation, your might to all who are to come (Ps. 71:17-18).

David realized the value in passing along what he knew to younger generations. He wanted other guys younger than him to sense God's power and might. A huge part of his life was dedicated to this. That's mentorship. The call as a man is to be a mentor and to continually seek out older guys willing to mentor you.

Really, mentorship needs to be a regular part of any spiritual leader's life. To this day, I (Shaun) have several mentors. My old youth pastor, Richard Clark, is one. We just talked a week ago. Growing up, he was always pouring truth into my life. When he became senior pastor of a church in Indiana, I worked with him for five years. Every chance I got, I learned from him. I worked at another church after that but always kept in close contact with Richard. I trust his perspective. He has become a pillar in my life. When Doug Fields called me about coming to Saddleback, Richard Clark was the first one I phoned.

One of my (Marcus's) mentors is Darell Smith, one of the head honchos with The Firs camping association. Darell's about 10 years older than I am, and we worked together several summers at camp. He's been there for me in various seasons of my life. He's given me advice on church situations, on girlfriends before I was married, on marriage and child-rearing today. Whenever we talk, he continually shifts the conversation to God. I totally admire that about him.

This mindset is what Paul encourages Timothy to do in 1 Timothy 4:12. The older pastor tells the younger:

> Don't let anyone look down on you because you are young, but set an example for the believers in speech, in life, in love, in faith and in purity.

Mentorship is about setting an example. At its core, it requires a mindset shift. No matter where you are or what you do, you look at the next generation of guys as people you can help.

DEVELOPING YOUR CODE
Formal / Informal Mentorship

What will being a mentor look like in your life? Maybe it will be a formal sort of mentorship where you meet with someone and regularly build into his life. When I (Shaun) was in college, there was a high school kid I mentored this way. We met every Wednesday at McDonalds and had coffee and chatted. It was good, honest talk, not contrived. The mentorship was set up through my church. The kid approached me and asked to be mentored.

Or maybe the mentorship will occur more subtly. When I (Marcus) was about 23, I was home late at night when a commercial came on television for Compassion International, the child relief agency. It showed these kids overseas picking through a garbage dump, looking for enough to eat. I wanted to be part of a system that saw the world's children as a good mentor would—that every man is called to help lead the next generation with honor and compassion.

So I sponsored a child. It only cost about 20 bucks a month back then. It's not much more now. That kid I sponsored grew up and graduated from high school; so I sponsored another, and he grew up through the system. My wife and I are sponsoring our third child now. I'd like to think of that as a type of mentorship—caring about the next generation.

We don't mean for this chapter to be the final word on mentoring. Rather, we simply hope to encourage you in this area, both to find good mentors throughout your life and to be a mentor wherever you can, no matter what age you're at.

With that in mind, let's do some work right now on this code. Work through these questions by yourself, with a small group of trusted guys, or one on one with a mentor.

1. What does it mean to be a mentor?

2. Why is it a good thing to develop a lifelong practice of being a mentor?

3. What are some different ways you can mentor younger guys around you?

Note
1. David Benjamin, "Getting Rich on a $20,000 Salary," *Kiplinger's Personal Finance Magazine*, September 7, 2007. http://articles.moneycentral.msn.com/Investing/StartInvesting/GettingRichOnA 20000DollarSalary.aspx (accessed October 2007).

ONE THING TO THINK ABOUT:

SEEK MENTORS AND BECOME A MENTOR.

DEVELOP YOUR CODE FROM HERE.

CHISELED
THE LASTING CODE OF SPIRITUAL MATURITY

My (Shaun's) youth staff just got back from a planning retreat. At the start of the weekend, we headed to the Anaheim Hyatt where the retreat was being held, and one of the younger guys on my staff decided to yell his name so that he could hear his echo. The Anaheim Hyatt is a palatial, four-star edifice—definitely not the type of place you want to make a scene. But my staff member hauled back his head and let loose—

RODNEY!!!!!

RO-O-O-O-O-O-O-D NAY!!! WHHHHOOOOOO.

Again, his name isn't Rodney, but you get the picture. All I could think was, *Dude, I just want to get away from you.*

Later that night, all the staff dined at Buca di Beppo, an Italian eatery where all the best Taralli and Cannelloni and marinated zucchini and Shrimp Capri is heaped high, brought to the center of the table, and placed on a revolving tray called a lazy Susan. The food swivels around so that everybody can dish up family style. Whenever people tried to get food, this same staff member nudged the lazy Susan—just for "fun." His joke went on and on. He guffawed his head off. I thought, *People just want to eat, and you're being a moron.*

At the end of the meal, this same guy and the guy next to him started a contest to see how far they could catapult calamari from their spoons. Flying squid. Circus squid. Airborne Squid. It was maybe funny the first time, but probably better suited to a summer camp lunchroom than the dinner table at a planning retreat. In the end, a piece of calamari landed on another guy's pants, leaving a grease stain. He wasn't happy.

My staff member just didn't know when to stop. Throughout the weekend, other jokes of his were received as warmly as sardines at a perfume convention. As his mentor, I should have pulled the guy aside after a while and said something to him, but when a guy is being a continual goof-off, it's difficult to know exactly what immature action to confront. And true, sometimes you just have to let people be people, and let the consequences of their actions be the best teacher.

I hope that's what happened in this case. I hope this guy got the hint. After a weekend together, it was clear that none of the 15 people on staff wanted to be around this guy much longer. Aside from his fellow calamari cohort, I noticed other staff members avoiding him.

For me, and the goals I had for the retreat, I felt that his immaturity had caused a lack of ease and changed the group dynamic of our time together. His actions caused people to be on edge, even to withdraw from each other. It frustrated our conversation. It wasted time. The end result: If this guy ever wanted to be successful in his ministry goals, if he wanted to be a productive, contributing member of the team, if he wanted to get along with people on anything more than a junior high level, he needed to grow up.

But here's where I'm gracious with this guy: As we've talked about all through this book, growing up is a lifelong process, not an instantaneous transaction. So maybe I needed to bust this guy's chops for being such a moron, but on the other hand, maybe I didn't need to do anything except pray for him and look for an open moment when I could talk to him. I know that down deep this guy's an all right guy. He has dedicated himself to following the Lord. He's in a good environment that cares for him and cares about his growth. He's going to grow up in his time and his way, and perhaps that's a bit slower than some guys, but that's okay.

The key to becoming truly mature as a man is not about putting yourself in the pressure cooker and getting an ulcer. Maturity happens as you continually choose to follow God.

That's part of what we want to talk about in this last chapter: God's table. Your invitation is to tuck a napkin around your neck, slide your chair in close and dig in.

CHISELED TRAINING
No More Soggy Fish

Think about God's table like this:

Guys (and men) seldom gravitate toward foreign films, particularly if they're subtitled. (Who wants to *read* a movie?) But there's one foreign film that's worth digging around for and watching with an eye to its greater meaning. It's called *Babette's Feast,* and sorry to say, there are no car chases, battle scenes, decapitations, dudes hanging off cliffs or wizards flying around on broomsticks. This movie demands that you think a bit. Fortunately, it's about food—and as guys we're pretty sure you can relate with that. But really, the movie is about much more than lunch. It's a metaphor for lasting spiritual maturity, which is also the last code we want to talk about in this book.

The movie presents two old, unmarried sisters who have grown up with a very rigid type of religion. They live on a cold, gray hill in Norway. They've shunned their chances at passion and fame. They're living out their lives singing joyless hymns, dutifully doing acts of charity and eating a diet that consists mostly of soggy fish soaked in water.

Along comes a French chef named Babette, who lives with the sisters for 14 years. At the end of that time, Babette wins the lottery and uses all her money to make one incredibly sumptuous dinner for the sisters and their stern church congregation.

The sisters and all the rigid folks are skeptical of the meal at first. They act frightened, high-handed and even suspicious of being offered such a feast. But they decide to dine anyway. They cautiously taste, then drink, then take another bite, then they eat some more. Wow, this food is good! The banquet works its magic. Babette's feast renews friendships, settles quarrels and revives the community's harmony. In the end, no one can ignore the transcendent power that the feast has brought to the town.

How is this movie about spiritual maturity?

It's easy to think of God as anything except good. Following Him is about duty, not joy. He's sullen and angry. His generosity can't be trusted. God is in our lives to make things difficult. He spanks us when we mess up. He busts our chops when we stray from the narrow path. When we decide to live for Him, we need to tighten our chests, suck up our dreams and put our noses to the grindstone. Surely that's what it must mean to live for God: Work hard. Work miserably. Have no fun. Spend the rest of your days eating soggy fish soaked in water.

The Bible offers a different perspective. Life with God is compared to a feast, freely given, where the best sorts of food are offered:

> Come, all you who are thirsty, come to the waters; and you who have no money, come, buy and eat! Come, buy wine and milk without money and without cost. . . . Listen, listen to me, and eat what is good, and your soul will delight in the richest of fare (Isa. 55:1-2).

The richest of fare. That's God's offering. Following Him is like sitting down to a table piled high with every food you love: barbecued ribs, steak, seven-layer burritos, hero sandwiches, cheeseburgers, Mom's meatloaf, cheesecake, donuts, apple pie and ice cream. You come to the table hungry and dine deep. Somebody else picks up the tab.

We're not talking about gluttony here. We're talking about the sumptuousness of following Christ. It's not a life of eating sour pickles. Sometimes following Christ can be difficult, challenging—there's that whole "take up your cross and follow me" part (Mark 8:34-35)—yet it's a life of purpose, adventure, heroics and strength. There is no better life.

How can you be truly mature as a man? It happens repeatedly when you decide to dine at His table. It happens continually when you choose to follow Him wholeheartedly, forever.

GETTING PUNCHED
Food and Fighting

There are a million images of God that lose their impact in translation to young men. *God's a gentle shepherd.* Who's interested in following a mild-mannered farm worker? *God's the lover of your soul.* Sounds a bit flighty, if you ask us. A lot of the images of Christ work best when connecting with children, women or old folks. But following Christ is a way of life for young men too. The aim is not to create a male-dominated church. Rather, Christianity is about living with a faith that values risk above safety, change over status quo, expansion over preservation and adventure over predictability. Following Christ is not about being a nice guy, a sort of sweater-wearing polite dude. It's about a purpose and challenge, an experience that matters, a risk-taking, fun-loving, often-dangerous-yet-victorious mission.

What if the image of God you carried in your head was of the toughest street fighter around? Or what if you pictured God as an Army first lieutenant, leading the charge through bullet-strewn crossfire? Or what if God was viewed as the right tackle on a professional football team? We're not trying to be stupid or irreverent here. We're just making a case for God's character and personality that you might not have imagined before. We want you to stop thinking about Christ the way He's often presented—as a long-haired boyfriend—and start thinking of Him as your Commander, Coach and Leader. Jesus Christ is a powerful hero who does great things. Following Him means standing up to danger, bearing up under suffering and sacrificing yourself for the good of others. Christ is the true Wildman, the King, the Warrior, the Judge and the Outlaw. Following Him is not for the fainthearted; it's for the tough, the stealthy and the brave.

The ancient patriarch Jacob meets this type of God. Or rather, God meets him. Funny, but God doesn't connect with Jacob at a committee meeting, a potluck or even at a Sunday morning service. God connects with Jacob in a fight. Genesis 32:22-32 records the battle. God appears in the form of a wrestler who throws arm barbs, cross hooks, and face busters at Jacob for about 12 hours. Jacob fights for all he's worth—he throws back his own chokeholds, dropkicks, and pile drivers at Christ. Think about it. Can you imagine smacking Christ across the face with a closed fist? This was no quiet game of Checkers these two were playing. Their fight was real and physical. It was single-combat, hand-to-hand fighting. A sweaty, bloody, spit-smearing brawl.

The result? Jacob won't give up, lose or quit—following Christ is never about becoming a doormat. Jacob's personality is headstrong. His life to this point has demonstrated nothing but arrogance, deception and pride. Christ refuses to beat Jacob on the man's own terms, so Christ throws a wrench into things and wounds Jacob's hip socket. Jacob finally encounters Someone he cannot defeat, and he finds out that the only way you get anywhere with God is by yielding to Him. Jacob changes his tune from fighting the Wrestler, to asking for the Wrestler's blessing. As a blessing, God changes Jacob's name—previously, Jacob's been known as a deceiver. The name change signifies an identity change as well. Jacob is now called Israel: someone who has wrestled with God, or "the champion of God," or "God fights." The name change means that Jacob won't be fighting under his own steam anymore. God would join Jacob in the fight.

It's a bit of a strange story, so let's put this into today's terms. There's a certain kind of guy who continually fights against God. He does the opposite of whatever God wants. God meets this type of guy exactly where he is. God's aim is not to destroy such a guy; it's to bless him, to give him a new name and identity. What's the new identity all about? Lifelong spiritual maturity. Much of life is a fight, yet God joins men in the fight. God's fight is about battling for the things that matter: justice, the end of oppression, reconciliation, the restoration of true self-worth. He battles for all that is good. That's the type of God we're called to follow.

TRUE TOUGHNESS
A Plan for the Long Haul

Lifelong spiritual maturity is like a banquet of your favorite foods.

Lifelong spiritual maturity means following a Commander who's with you in the battle.

What else?

There's one last verse we'd like to leave you with. It's my (Marcus's) life verse, and it means a lot to Shaun as well. It's Psalm 16:8:

I have set the LORD always before me. Because He is at my right hand, I will not be shaken.

That's what male maturity is all about: setting the Lord always before you. It's true toughness, a lifetime of unswervingly following Christ. It's not a decision you make today and then forget about and do your own thing. You choose to follow Christ daily. Forever.

So many guys out there are fighting to be real men. They swagger, and buy stuff they don't need, and have sex with a string of girls they don't care about, and live a life of basic meaninglessness, all because they're hoping for something that matters. But becoming a real man only happens when you commit to following Christ. Maturity happens when you set the Lord always before you—in front of you to follow, in first place of priorities and out front as the point person of reference. It's when you give Him His rightful place in your life at all times.

That's the last thought we'd like to leave you with. We hope that you feel we've walked alongside you through this journey. We haven't arrived yet. We're with you in this. We started this book by talking about the differences in maturity that we can sense inwardly. The older we get, the more we don't want to be considered *guys* anymore. We know that we need to make the transition to the next stage of life, but we're not sure who we need to become, how to get there or even how to start the process.

We talked about how this book is not a call to act older than you are right now. Age and maturity are not the same thing. If you're 18, we want you to be 18. If you're 25, we want you to be 25. There are things you can do at 18 or 25 that you can never do the rest of your life.

We talked about how no one is going to force you to become mature. It's something only you can decide you want—but who wouldn't want to develop this type of true toughness? Maturity is something that will ultimately benefit you in the end. It's in your best interest to keep pressing on toward maturity. When you're mature, it means that you can handle whatever life throws at you. You have the inside knowledge and resolve to know how to really live. When the punches of life come your way, you won't break, crumble or shake apart.

So that's why this book is called *Chiseled*. What does that mean? Chiseled is a process as much as it's an end result. God chisels a person—He shapes and molds that person into maturity. When you're chiseled, the things that are flabby or immature or unneeded in your life are honed away. You're the man God made you to be.

Here's that great verse again that puts maturity into perspective:

When I was a child, I talked like a child, I thought like a child, I reasoned like a child. When I became a man, I put childish ways behind me (1 Cor. 13:11).

That's the maturity we've been talking about throughout this book. Putting childish (or *guy-ish*) ways behind you. The older you get, the more you don't want to be naïve or goofy, someone who's gullible, foolish or easily influenced. You want to develop a wise, skillful approach to living. That's true toughness; that's what it means to be mature.

Can you do it?

Absolutely. When you know and respect the codes for being a man, you have the principles that guide you into the life you were meant to lead. In a sense, you approach life with a diamond jaw, a chin made from the world's hardest substance. You can take all the punches life throws at you. You've got the necessary tools to develop the codes.

So what's your next step?

We want to encourage you to start slow and start real. Maturity isn't developed overnight. But this is your invitation right now. Become mature—don't settle for anything less. Start to develop your codes. Learn a wise, skillful approach to living, and become the man of God you were meant to be.

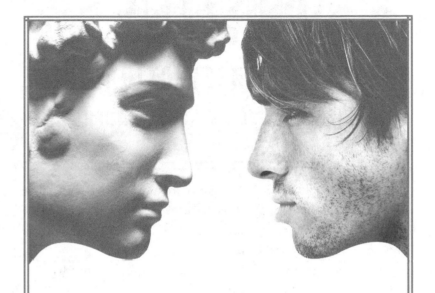

ONE THING TO THINK ABOUT:

SET THE LORD ALWAYS BEFORE YOU.

DEVELOP YOUR CODE FROM HERE.

CHISELED

DISCUSSION / REFLECTION GUIDE
(WITH HELP FOR GROUP LEADERS)

Thanks for reading this book. We've included some discussion points and going-deeper ideas here because we want to help you think and talk through the ideas in Chiseled. You can use this section alone or in a group.

If you're a group leader, here are some quick reminders:

- Encourage everyone to individually read through all of *Chiseled*. You might want to have them do this all at once before you start the study, or you can read a chapter each week. Stay open to whatever questions the group members have as a result of interacting with the content.

- Various questions and opinions will undoubtedly come up. That's okay. Whenever possible, have the group search the Scriptures together to look for God's answers and perspective. Use the Bible to keep God's wisdom in charge of your discussion.

- Set an example by responding honestly to the themes of *Chiseled*. All of us have a lot of room to grow in learning how to live out this book's ideas. So be candid about your personal needs. As you face your group honestly, you'll be encouraging others in your group to do the same.

· Pray with and for your group members. Ask God to be at work in their lives, and thank Him ahead of time (by faith) for what He will do.

· As you pray, ask God to protect your group from disunity, selfishness and pride. Ask the Holy Spirit to give all of you spiritual insight into His truths from Scripture. Ask for personal discoveries and break-throughs in each person's life.

CHAPTER 1—FACEDOWN

THE BIG IDEA

Facedown is the attitude of bowing your heart to God and letting Him work in your life. All maturity begins here.

The goal in becoming mature is not that anyone would simply *act* wiser. You don't need to buckle down, shape up, shine up your life, or grit your teeth and try harder. Jesus scorned people who were only interested in changing behaviors without changing their core.

True maturity is an issue of changing the heart—of changing inner motivations, tendencies and leanings. It's when we become wiser from the inside out. And that only happens when we're facedown before God.

TALK ABOUT IT

1. What's one way that you've acted immature in the past? Give some stories.

2. In the book, you read that developing maturity at a heart level depends on two things: (1) the power of God in your life, and (2) the choices you make, which demonstrate your willingness to let God's power change you. What does this mean—i.e., how does a person ultimately become mature?

3. Read Proverbs 1:1-7. What are some of the benefits of becoming mature? At the same time, what are some of the consequences if a person doesn't become mature?

4. Read Proverbs 1:7 again—just the one verse. What does it mean (or not mean) to "fear" the Lord? Give a practical example of how a young man might fear the Lord.

5. Shaun and Marcus give some practical examples of living life facedown as a practical means of demonstrating wisdom. How about you—have you ever been in a situation when you could have done either a mature or an immature thing, and you chose to follow Christ? How did things resolve, if they did? What do you think God might want you to learn from that experience?

CHAPTER 2—INTERNET NANTUCKET

THE BIG IDEA

If you don't have self-control, life hurts. It's as simple as that. Maybe life hurts now; or maybe life will hurt later, when the results of living by impulse catch up with you. One way or another it's a simple formula: Lack of self-control equals pain.

Only with self-control can you live the life you truly want to live. Having self-control means that you focus every thought and action on your most important goals, then slice away your lesser wants.

Self-control is an exchange; you exchange your impulses for your greater goals.

TALK ABOUT IT

1. What's one area of your life in which you've acted on impulse, and regretted it later? What's one area in which you've acted with self-control, and benefited?

2. In the book, you read: *The crazy thing about living a life that's in God's control is that God never asks you to relinquish responsibility either. It's God's* ultimate *control working in harmony with our* personal *control. God's in charge, yet we are always responsible for our actions.* What does this mean? How does a person's will and God's will work in tandem? (Hint: Read Gal. 5:16-25.)

3. Read Titus 2:1-8. What's significant about the fact that Paul has only one directive for young men?

4. What's true accountability, and why does every guy need it?

5. What are the top areas right now where your struggle with self-control is greatest? Can you give an example? What steps do you need to take today to ensure success in this area?

CHAPTER 3—STEEL GIRDERS

THE BIG IDEA

Integrity means that your life demonstrates an uncompromising adherence to ethical principles. You show such qualities as forthrightness and straightforwardness. Integrity is a state of being whole or entire. It's a diamond-solid life, a life that doesn't crack under intense pressure. Integrity shows soundness, an ability to deliver on promises. Think of integrity as a refusal to be false, or a pledge to be upright. It's what you want the people around you to have. It's what you absolutely need in your own life to become the man you want to be.

Developing integrity is not a one-time decision; it's a way of life, or a series of decisions you continually make. It means constantly aligning your heart with what you know is true, noble, pure, admirable and right.

TALK ABOUT IT

A person's integrity can show up (or crack) in a lot of different ways. What are some examples you've seen of integrity (or lack of it)?

1. Solomon spoke a lot about integrity, but his life crumbled at the end. Why do you think this happened? How could a man who was so wise blow it?

2. Read this somewhat long passage of Scripture—Job 1–2. How does Job demonstrate integrity? What do his wife and his friends tempt him to do?

3. At its core, integrity is a heart thing. Read Matthew 5:27-28 and Matthew 6:5-6. What did the Pharisees

think integrity meant? How did Jesus define having integrity?

4. What are the areas in which you struggle the most with integrity? What steps do you need to take today (maybe every day) to ensure true maturity in this area?

CHAPTER 4—APPLAUDING ESTHER

THE BIG IDEA

Real chivalry is a heart attitude of admiration—it begins in your thoughts, attitudes and motivations. If people all over the world can applaud for stuff like football games, dessert or airplane landings, then why not applaud for something as important as the opposite gender? It doesn't mean actually slapping your hands together whenever you see a girl. It's all about treating women with respect, praise, appreciation and acclaim. In a word—it's *applause.*

Real chivalry means that you root for someone's goals and ambitions. You cheer for what they find important. When it comes to the women in your life, it means honoring their character, heart, achievement and whole person. Chivalry wraps around courtesy and consideration. It embraces courage and bravery. It requires valor and respect—all the character traits you want to develop in your journey to become a real man.

TALK ABOUT IT

1. What are some ways that guys treat women poorly? What have you seen?

2. Why is chivalry a good thing? Why treat women with the utmost respect?

3. Read Genesis 2:18-25. The Bible says that it's not good for a man to be alone. What does this look like in everyday life today? Are there occasions when it's okay for a guy to be alone? How about long-term? Why do you think you need women in your life?

4. Shaun and Marcus talk about several "punches" when it comes to guys' attitudes toward women: lust, dating ambition, fear, insecurity, passivity, dating to play around, preoccupation and "the goofball" punch. What punch, or punches, do you think you struggle with the most? Give some examples.

5. Read 1 Timothy 5:1-2 and Ephesians 5:25. Basically, chivalry boils down to three areas: treating older women as mothers, treating younger women as sisters, and loving your wife, or future wife. What steps do you need to take today (maybe every day) to ensure true maturity in this area?

CHAPTER 5 — BANDED

THE BIG IDEA

If you're a young man and attend church right now, chances are that in a year or two you won't. For some reason, church and youth group connect with high school guys, but college guys drop out.

Why is this lame? It means you'll pass through your most formative years as a young adult with your Christianity on the backburner. All the life-shaping decisions of that decade—to finish college or not, what career to pursue, where to live, whether to get married, who you marry, whether to have children, and many more decisions, get made outside the context of spiritual community

Church is for training and service. It's to shape and mold you.

TALK ABOUT IT

1. Why is it important that young men connect with a church?

2. What are some of the challenges young men face when they go to church? Why is it sometimes hard to go? The phrase a lot of people use to bail on church is "church just doesn't meet my needs." Why might this be a flawed perspective of what church is all about?

3. Read Ephesians 4:11-16. Shaun and Marcus make this statement: "We don't *go* to church. We *are* the church." What does this mean?

4. One of the main purposes of a worship service is to connect with God. If you find yourself in a worship service, and there's something happening that you don't like, how might you connect with God anyway?

5. Church is not simply a place we attend—we are the church, and our call is to serve, or minister, to others. Sometimes ministry happens within the walls of a church building, but often it happens elsewhere. What type of ministry do you sense you're called to?

CHAPTER 6 — QUEUED

THE BIG IDEA

When you work haphazardly or lackadaisically or with a surly attitude, you rob yourself of life's good stuff: the ability to work as God intended. Having a strong work ethic means being professional, being diligent in your work and being a team player with the people around you. But it's also more than that. God knows that whenever you take what He's given you and use it for good, you benefit. He delights whenever you delight in the talents and abilities you've been given. God and work and being a man are closely intertwined. So when you work, you actually reflect something of the way God made you.

TALK ABOUT IT

1. The chapter opens with these lines: "It used to be that the customer was always right. These days it seems, the customer's just an annoyance." Have you seen examples of this—where people have a poor work ethic, and it shows?

2. What are some jobs you've done that you didn't like? How might those experiences have been good? That is, did you learn something? Did you accomplish something you can put on your résumé? What else?

3. Read Luke 19:11-27. The point of the parable of the talents is that everyone has different abilities and gifts. God asks you to use what you've been given. Work well and live well no matter where you are, even if it's the off-season or if you only have one talent. That's having a strong work ethic. In the Bible pas-

sage, why do you think the king reacted so strongly to the guy who buried his talents (vv. 22-23)? Why is it important to use the talents you've been given?

4. Read Genesis 39:1-3; 39:22-23; 41:39-46. Joseph was a slave and a prisoner before he rose to second-in-command of all Egypt. What was Joseph's perspective about any job he had?

5. In what career direction are you heading? What are some of the obstacles you expect to encounter along the way? What type of job can you see yourself doing long-term? What greater purpose do you think that job has?

CHAPTER 7—BANKED

THE BIG IDEA

Everything in your life belongs to God. It's all His. Whether it's your family, your friends, your finances or your future—if you clutch something, it's bound to get squished.

Only when you release what you have back to Him does life make sense.

Yet money can't be ignored. We're to seek God's kingdom and His righteousness first, but that doesn't mean we're to be ignorant about money or how it works. Christ always calls us to live a life of wisdom and faith.

TALK ABOUT IT

1. What are some problems that guys can have with money? Describe some examples you've seen or heard of.

2. Shaun and Marcus talk about three main punches that come at young men: (1) depreciating assets, such as new cars and electronic goods, are heavily marketed toward you, (2) credit is pushed on you but you're seldom shown how to use it wisely, and (3) it's easy to overlook learning how to manage money wisely. What's the hardest thing about money for you right now, and what are you going to do about it?

3. Read Luke 12:15-21. "Money is only a tool." What does this mean?

4. Read Luke 12:22-34. What does it mean to be both wise and faithful when it comes to money?

5. Think about finances in these categories: spending, saving, budgeting, investing, credit, tithing. Talk about each category—what is your responsibility in each? What is one step you can take this week toward greater overall financial responsibility?

CHAPTER 8 — LONG-HAUL FAITH

THE BIG IDEA

If you want to have true fervor for the life God invites you to lead, you can't ignore tomorrow. You've got to develop your code of best practices. Consider these the disciplines that let you move beyond running sprints to running all-out marathons. Primarily, these disciplines relate to three sides of your life: physical, mental (which often includes emotional) and spiritual. The big question here is, How can you succeed over the long haul?

TALK ABOUT IT

1. Why is it necessary to think not only about today but also about the long term?

2. Why are Christians often notorious for ignoring the disciplines that ensure their long-term sustainability and success?

3. Read Mark 6:31-32; Mark 4:38; Luke 3:23; Luke 6:12. Talk about the life of Christ. What are some of the disciplines He developed that showed a life in balance?

4. Read Daniel 1. How might your life be similar to a young man in Babylon, and what resolves might you need to ensure your success in your culture?

5. What "best practice" do you currently succeed at most? In which area do you struggle most? What is something you can do this week to help develop one best practice in your life?

CHAPTER 9 — BROTHERS

THE BIG IDEA

Every man is called to be a model for, and to lead, the next generation with honor, wisdom and compassion. To become mature, you will want to have mentors and you will want to be one yourself. Viewing the next generation with an eye to guidance is something you can do your whole life.

TALK ABOUT IT

1. What does it mean to be a mentor?

2. Often there's a mental shift required when we begin to view the people around us within a mentorship grid. As young men, we're typically expected to scoff at younger guys, almost to bully them. What are some ways you've seen this principle in action? Has it ever happened to you? Why might it not be the best practice for viewing guys younger than yourself?

3. Read Exodus 17:8-15 and 18:13-27. Moses mentored Joshua, and Jethro mentored Moses. Why is it necessary to both have a mentor and be a mentor?

4. What qualities do you seek in a mentor? If you don't have a mentor, how might you go about getting one?

5. Talk about the difference between formal and informal mentorships. What are some different ways that you can mentor younger guys around you?

CHAPTER 10 — CHISELED

THE BIG IDEA

In this final chapter, we ask: How can you be truly mature as a man? Three thoughts are given: You show maturity when you (1) decide to dine at God's lavish table, (2) follow Him as your commander, and (3) choose to set Him in His rightful place and follow Him wholeheartedly forever.

TALK ABOUT IT

1. When you think about following Christ for the rest of your life, what thoughts come to mind? Does this idea challenge and inspire you, or does it feel like a big drag, something you could take or leave.

2. Picture your life three years from now. How old will you be? What might you be doing? Where might you be living? What do you hope your life will be like? What do you hope your relationship with God will be like?

3. Read Genesis 32:22-32. What does it mean that God meets us in a fight?

4. Read Psalm 16:8. What does it look like to set the Lord always before you?

5. Spend some time in prayer as a group, asking the Lord to develop the code of maturity in your lives.

ACKNOWLEDGMENTS

From Shaun:

I want to thank several people that have been a part of the chiseling process in my life, as well as a help, encouragement and sounding board through the writing of this book.

Thanks to my parents for raising me in a God-filled environment, Ron and Beth Blakeney. Thanks to my sister, Shannon, for letting me be a "guy" in all our years growing up.

Thanks to Richard Clark, minister, mentor, teacher and friend. Thanks also to Doug Fields for all you've done for me.

Thanks to my agent Greg Johnson, editor Steven Lawson and everyone at Regal Publishing. Thanks to my honest reading friends, Cody Moran and Jeff Baker.

From Marcus:

My heartfelt thanks go to the numerous people who have encouraged me throughout life, as well as in the writing of this book.

Thanks to my parents and in-laws for your ever-present support, Graham and Dorothy Brotherton, Mike and Judy Albin. To Jon and Alison Brotherton, Japheth and Elly, David and Carrie Albin, thanks for your encouragement.

Thanks to David Kopp, professor, writing mentor, coach and friend. To mentors Darell Smith, Tim Johnson, Mike Johnson and Jon Aldrich. To pastor Brent Iseli—our lunchtime talks helped form this book.

Thanks to literary agent Greg Johnson, editors Steven Lawson, Deena Davis, Mark Weising, and the team at Regal. Thanks to my readers on this project, DGB and HC Jones, and to Drew Johnson for your helpful feedback up front. Thanks to Randy Ingermanson (the Snowflake guy) for your teaching on best practices.

Thanks to Bob Craddock and Karen Clark, unswerving friends.

Please support:

Compassion International
www.compassion.com

The Mercy & Sharing Foundation
www.haitichildren.com

ABOUT THE AUTHORS

Shaun Blakeney serves as the student ministries pastor at Christ Fellowship in Palm Beach Gardens, Florida. Previously, he was the high school pastor at Saddleback Church for four years, where he co-wrote this book. Shaun holds a bachelor's degree from Florida Christian College and is currently finishing a master's degree from Indiana Wesleyan University. He has been a minister since 1992. In addition to his responsibilities at Christ Fellowship, Shaun ministers to thousands of young adults each year at conferences, seminars and festivals. He is a regular speaker at large-scale venues such as the Youth Specialties conventions and Willow Creek Community Church. Shaun is the co-founder of iyouthministry.com (a social network for youth pastors to connect, share and inspire). Shaun and his wife, Teresa, have two children, Austin and Alyssa, and live in south Florida.

Marcus Brotherton is an ordained minister and writer. He has authored or coauthored 16 books, including the acclaimed FlipSwitch series for teens. A former youth pastor and newspaper reporter, Marcus holds a master's degree from Talbot Seminary at Biola University and a bachelor's degree from Multnomah University, where he received the Evangelical Press Association award for top university writer in America. Marcus and his wife, Mary Margaret, have one daughter, Addy, and live in Washington State.